IT

TINA

NIALL HARBISON

TINA

THE DOG
WHO CHANGED
THE WORLD

HARPER
element

HarperElement
An imprint of HarperCollins*Publishers*
1 London Bridge Street
London SE1 9GF

www.harpercollins.co.uk

HarperCollins*Publishers*
Macken House, 39/40 Mayor Street Upper
Dublin 1, D01 C9W8, Ireland

First published by HarperElement 2025

All plate-section images courtesy of the author, with the exception of
page 4 (top) 'Tina's Hospital' © Danny Forster & Architecture

A catalogue record of this book is
available from the British Library

HB ISBN 978-0-00-872571-6 - Impression 3
Waterstones HB ISBN 978-0-00-877775-3 - Impression 2
PB ISBN 978-0-00-872572-3 - Impression 4

Printed and bound in the UK using 100%
renewable electricity at CPI Group (UK) Ltd

To Alba.

The world wasn't kind to you, but for 14 sunrises
you made me and people around the world dream,
smile and be kind.

This book is dedicated to you and all the street
dogs out there without a voice.

CONTENTS

PROLOGUE

It all starts, as so many dog rescues do, with my WhatsApp pinging.

A picture message.

I don't recognise the number it's been sent from, it's not from a friend or a member of the family back home. So I can be pretty sure that the image I've received will be of a dog – and it's probably not going to be a cute 'awww' kind of one.

In those few milliseconds as I wait for it to download, there's a familiar sense of dread of whatever's coming next. It wasn't long after getting sober that my mission to save the street dogs in Thailand began. I've grown used to the fact that I'm like the fourth emergency service out here. For humans there's the fire, ambulance and police services – for dogs, however, well, it's fair to say I've become the go-to in that department.

It seems to take an age for the image to become clear. Living in Koh Samui, a tropical island off the east coast of the country, has many wonderful things going for it – clear blue skies, fluffy white clouds and luscious jungles to explore. It even has some of the fastest WiFi in the world but today it was taking forever.

A little anxiety seeds in my tummy. *Come on then, how bad will it be?*

You'd imagine I'd get hardened to seeing upsetting pictures of mistreated animals after all this time. Some are cruelly abused by humans, others were just unlucky enough to be born. Unwanted and unloved by anyone. Suffering, because the world just isn't always fair.

Yet despite all the horrible states I've found animals in, I never get desensitised. I'm a big softie I suppose, there's always something that can still shock me, make me wince, or induce flashes of utter fury sometimes. (Never aimed at the poor wretched animal. I'm only ever angry at the humans who've neglected them – or, worse, maliciously inflicted the damage. Or just society as a whole for not caring as we should.)

As the picture on my iPhone finally crystallises with definition, turning from a blurry shape into a clear photo-graph, I see it's a dog on a chain. The fur is fair, thin and matted in places, while sparse in others; there's some expanses of sore-looking skin exposed. I peer closer and notice the poor thing has been lying in its own toileting. Eugh.

But the dog's face is long and noble somehow, and poking out from the fur obscuring the poor thing's vision are the most vulnerable-looking dark eyes I've ever seen.

The expression is of complete dejection, one of the saddest-looking animals I've ever seen. I groan audibly and put my head in my hands briefly.

It is impossible to tell the breed of the mutt from the picture, and let's be honest the 'breeds' in Thailand are way more loosely based on the intended breed. Most of the dogs out here in Koh Samui are a mix-up of all sorts as they've haphazardly mated on the street and multiplied (and multiplied, and multiplied ...). All sorts of doggy DNA exists, born by accident and not design.

And in my opinion they're just as beautiful as any pooch who might be showcased at glamorous dog shows like Crufts in the UK or the National Dog Show in the US. And their life is every bit as valuable. I just wish there weren't quite so many of them.

I read the rest of the text that follows the picture. This particular poor mite had been spotted by a tourist in the mountains earlier that morning. That part of the island isn't one I was so familiar with. I have to admit, I still don't know every corner of Koh Samui. (The fact that for the first couple of years of living in this paradise I was mostly steaming drunk definitely didn't help me in that regard.)

I rub my eyes again. *God, I'm knackered.* I want my dinner, I want a shower, and I want to curl up on the sofa with my own dog Snoop. But this is one of those moments when you just know you have to drop everything. *Just go, Niall.* I know in every bone of my body that here is a dog in dire need; he or she simply could not spend another night in that miserable dirty state.

Whoever it belongs to, and however it got there, I need to go and help it. Immediately.

I close down the message from the tourist on my phone, and quickly scroll through my contacts to find the number of my Aussie mate, Rod. When a dog rescue seems like it might be a complex one, Rod is the guy I call. And he picks up after three rings.

'Rod,' I announce, cutting short any pleasantries. 'I need your help, my friend, there's another dog that needs us right now – and I have a feeling this one won't be easy …'

CHAPTER ONE

THE RETRIEVAL OF OUR GOLDEN GIRL

Most of the dogs I come across could all do with a bit of TLC. They're in need of food in their belly, some basic medication to ward off parasites and a dollop of love, or at least attention, from a human. But some animals do stand out more than others. I'm not claiming to be Doctor Doolittle, or possess any special powers to 'talk to the animals' (if only I could, it would save a hell of a lot of hassle).

But if you yourself spend time with any dogs or other pets (and I'm guessing you might, if you've picked up this book) then you'll know where I'm coming from. You'll know yourself that you don't need to learn any new language to be able to read an animal's expression. Look into their eyes – what are they really trying to tell you? Watch their body language. Just like us humans, dogs all have a huge amount of feelings. And the best thing is they don't lie, or act up, like us complicated humans do.

They wear their doggy hearts on their paw-like sleeves and in the movement of their tails. And there was just something about that mournful, puppy dog face as it was shackled to a short chain that really got under my skin in particular, for some reason.

So to the mountains I headed that February afternoon, along with my trusty great pal Rod, who moved out here to retire from working in the police force, but because he's as passionate about animal welfare as I am, he seemed to work even harder now in his so-called retirement. We jumped in the truck and steadily made our way up the winding muddy tracks to the summit to see what was what. We skidded around a bit and I was definitely grateful I hadn't attempted the trek on my moped. I was also bracing myself. My instinct wasn't good for what awaited us.

It took us about 20 minutes to find the mountain shack where the dog was chained. Asking locals for directions isn't always that helpful, and I'm ashamed to admit I'm not exactly fluent in Thai. So there was a fair bit of peering at the picture to see what backgrounds we could recognise, and some being pointed off in the wrong direction, until finally we found the spot. *Bingo.*

On reaching the shack we saw it was more like a basic wooden house, with an open basement part beneath the main structure. And inside that basement area, we found the sorriest sight you can imagine. However bad an impression is in a picture, it's always even more heartbreaking to be confronted with the living, breathing animal having to just put up with their miserable situation.

This one, curled up and tethered on a chain that was barely two metres long, was one of the most tragic I'd seen. The dog was dozing as we walked in, and as I quickly took in the dingy surroundings and inhaled the dank smell of the shack, well, I couldn't help wondering if here in front of me was a dog thinking whether it might not be the worst thing never to wake up at all. There wasn't much incentive to keep going if this was your lot in life.

I know all too well the feeling. Many times in my life I had felt this way in the low and dark corners of my mind. As if I had nothing going for me at all. Like life has exhausted you and sucked you dry.

But as I inched a little closer to the dozing creature, she stirred from her slumber.

I could spot some teats on her tummy, so it was clearly a female bitch, and she didn't seem that old (though it can be hard to tell until a vet trip and a look at her teeth). She had the biggest, softest brown eyes I've ever seen.

There was a quiet pleading expression in her dark eyes which begged, 'Help me, do something to help me here, Niall.'

Poor little sweetheart. I crouched down gingerly to stroke her head – but there was no flinching. She looked me directly in the eyes. Kind dark eyes, with a real soul inside them. What's more, she didn't seem at all scared of human touch, though God knows she certainly hadn't been on the receiving end of much of that, from the look of things. She even gratefully nuzzled into my arm as I carried on stroking her, as if to say, 'Please don't leave me here, give me a hand.'

She was an absolute bag of bones – every rib on her little body seemed visible. Clearly it had been a long time since she'd got a decent dinner in her belly. There was a plastic container of water which wasn't exactly fresh, but must have been enough to keep her going. *Jesus*, I muttered under my breath. *What the hell has happened for her to wash up here?*

What I always do in these situations is to try and find out as much as I can about a dog's backstory. Any information you can gather about *how* they wound up in this state, might then help you give them the right kind of medical support that they need. Of course I'd love to know *why* she had ended up here too, but I'd long learned that wasn't always possible.

You so rarely get the truth. People you meet – and ask – are generally defensive, knowing in their heart that they've not done the right thing. Even if that person is not directly responsible for putting the dog in this misery, well, then they certainly know that they haven't helped either. So I was prepared to be fed one of the bullsh*t kind of stories I hear all the time.

There were 'owners' around, apparently, but no one was taking any responsibility. Someone said the dog had been hit by a car, and had then been tied up 'for her own safety'. Others suggested she was old and injured, though quite why that would mean she should be left tied up here I never understood. People mainly don't want to lose face, and don't like an annoying Westerner asking questions. I am in no way trying to do anyone down, especially being a foreigner in this country, but not 'losing face' is a really big deal in the culture. And I need to understand and respect that, even if it leaves me confused.

Whatever the real story, I could only work with the reality in front of my eyes. Here was a female dog, who was tied to a chain which allowed her only the length to jump up a bit and go to the loo. And not even that far really – the poor thing was surrounded by her own poo and wee. Neither hygienic, fair on her, or remotely dignified – sleeping surrounded by her own mess is just horrible.

The floor was concrete, and there were some random dirty buckets lying around and an old green towel that I suppose might have originally been placed there to offer some respite from the hard floor. Or perhaps had been used to mop up the mess, and then no one could be bothered to wash it or even pick it up afterwards.

Jesus, what's wrong with people?

What happened next is now a very familiar scenario to me, when you open up 'negotiations' to take the dog away. I knew this 'owner', or whoever they were really, didn't want her anymore. Clearly! And they were actually hoping

I'd take the dog off their hands and be done with it. Their basement would be rid of her – as would their conscience, what little they might have had.

But no-one wants to lose face, and me trying to 'shame' anyone is of no real benefit in the long term. I know that may sound ridiculous to people reading this book back home in the UK, because there you'd call the RSPCA (Royal Society for the Protection of Animals), or even the police in situations like this. But I always have to remember things work differently in different parts of the world and in different cultures.

Confrontation is rarely the best approach. And I'm just not an aggressive person; there's no point getting mad or angry about the way the animals have been treated. It's much better to channel my energies in a more positive way – and to make a hands-on difference to dogs' lives.

Being diplomatic usually gets a better outcome, and the goal here is always to help the animal. *Be nice, Niall, be nice, smile and get the dog the hell out of there.*

With loyal and kind Rod next to me for moral support, we stepped outside of the basement to escape the dinge and I talked to the supposed owners. After some half-hearted persuasion, they agreed we could take her to the vet. I was relieved, but I knew the situation was still precarious. Much work lay ahead.

Once the owner had shrugged and left us to it, Rod and I went inside to get her, and the first thing we did was remove the tatty thing that she was tethered to; it seemed like a makeshift lead made of string and bits of rope. It had been shackling her down like a prisoner for God knows how long, and it was tricky to remove, especially as we didn't have any tools with us in the back of the jeep. What we desperately needed was a set of pliers but in the end we had to improvise a bit with some patience and brute force, yanking at the chain while making sure she felt nothing tugging at her. The rope was wrapped around her neck several times but somehow we managed to untie it from the wall and free her.

A small step, but a start.

The moment the dog was out of that tatty basement, it became clear just how dire her condition really was. She was pitifully weak and her horribly malnourished and neglected body broke me.

Her bones were sticking out so sharply that it was hard to believe she was still alive, and she could barely use her shaking four legs. It was clear she hadn't walked in a long time, and she was completely disoriented and uncoordinated. It was horribly sad to see. But what was even more heartbreaking to observe was this sort of look of utter confusion she had. Here she was off the chain and free to walk, yet her little legs seemed to have forgotten what they were there for.

By all rights, the creature should have been angry, bitter, aggressive and withdrawn. She kept shaking her head to test if it really *was* liberated from the neck restriction, not quite believing it was happening.

Yet the trusting little girl she was, she came with us right away, as if she could sense she was finally safe. I bent down to her level and stroked her head, looking into her eyes, amazingly entirely lacking in any suspicion. 'We've got you now, we're going to protect you, don't worry about that, my angel,' I soothed her.

I kept hold of her manky fur (I couldn't wait to get her clean) to make sure she was close to me, gently guiding her towards the jeep. Though there was no need really – she wouldn't have had the energy or strength to run away. And she also seemed to instinctively not want to. As if knowing that this was the turning point for her – and now life was looking up all of a sudden, she wasn't going anywhere, thank you.

As soon as we'd carefully lifted her skinny body onto the truck, we gently secured her, her little bemused face in the back seat looking out the window. We then put our foot down to get her to the vet before closing time.

I knew immediately that we needed at all costs an initial once-over from a professional to get the status of this dog's overall health. I have picked up a few tricks myself over the few years I've been doing this. I'd like to think I am a quick hand at treating certain health issues and am comfortable diagnosing ear infections and the odd scar but something told me this was out of my league, she was just too poorly looking. So her bloods were taken and I made a royal fuss of this sorry dog while we waited the 15 minutes for the results to come back.

Running my hands over the horribly neglected fur, I stroked and soothed her. And then it hit me – this little girl wasn't one of your regular-looking dogs we have out here. 'You know what,' I said out loud, looking at her with some surprise, 'I'm pretty sure you're a golden retriever aren't you, girl?' I like to think she wagged her tail a little bit in that moment.

This was far from the norm to come across a pedigree dog out here.

Golden retrievers, with their striking yellow coats, are beautiful breeds of dog, renowned for their gentle and affectionate natures. So much so, that in many Western countries, they're often the breeds chosen to train as guide dogs because they're so lovely and caring. Not to mention adorable to look at. This poor one in front of me, however, was covered in sores from living on a hard concrete floor. And there wasn't much 'golden' about the grotty condition of her coat at that time.

When the blood results came back the vet was frowning. 'This dog has obviously been neglected for a very long time,' he said, shaking his head. He confirmed she was in a terrible shape: blood parasites, severe anaemia, and all her vital signs were dangerously low because she was so frail. Her weight was just 12.5 kg or 25 lb, way under what a normal dog of her sex, age and breed should be.

It also seemed there was a potential issue with her kidneys, and more tests would be needed later down the line, said the vet. It made no sense to me that this dog was a rare pedigree breed and someone must have once paid a lot for her. Why would they then not take care of her? Why had she been effectively left to rot and die?

I couldn't work it out, but the vet speculated that, because of her pedigree and unusual looks (being fair haired is seen as 'exotic' here), the poor thing had likely been acquired and then used for breeding purposes. Her exhausted body, explained the vet, pointing to her teats, showed the evidence of having had many litters. Adult retrievers can have up to three litters a year, and each litter produces on average six or seven puppies. I have no idea what they might have charged for each one, but you can see how greed might have played a part.

This nameless, helpless creature in front of me had been exploited as a money-making scheme – used and abused to have countless batches of puppies at the hand of some mercenary human. Once she had served her purpose, after her body had endured immense stress from having so many puppies, she had carelessly been discarded.

It made me well up thinking of how awful her life must have been. I've seen first-hand so many times the wonderful, natural mothering instinct female animals seem to have. Only a few months earlier, I'd rescued a dog called Beyoncé, who was so fiercely protective of her six little pups that she'd kept them hidden, going on the hunt for food, which she'd binge and then cleverly manage to regurgitate and feed them herself once she felt she was in a hidden safe place to do it. Animals have such caring and protective instincts when it comes to their young.

This dog here would have had the same maternal desire to nurture her pups, yet instead they would have been taken away from her, in what would have been a painful and bewildering loss for her. Time and again.

The vet gave me some basic medicines to address the parasites, which meant we could at least sort out the more superficial irritations for her, like mange and other skin infections.

We left the vet's and drove her down Hope Avenue. For those of you who might not be familiar with our story, Hope Avenue is a very special road. It started out as a dirt track in the middle of the jungle. To be more precise it was just a field in the jungle but it is a path that myself and some of the dogs use to walk along to get them some exercise. Slowly a little path started to form and eventually I was able to drive my moped along it.

Eventually we got gravel put down and planted some tiny trees that have since blossomed into the most beautiful yellow tall trees that complement the greens of the jungle and the vast bright blue skies above us. What was once a little path in the jungle now symbolises our mission, and as soon as we reach Hope Avenue with a very sick dog in tow we know they are entering a doggy paradise and a place where their sickness and abuse has ended and their recovery can start.

As soon as we turned down the path, I felt a sigh of relief. Once back we got a big plastic tub, filled it with soapy water and gave her a much needed wash. We do this for every rescue dog that ends up at the land and there is always a moment while the street dogs adjust to this new situation. But this dog, she stood there – good as gold – while we cleaned her gently with warm water, getting rid of all the nasty bits of poo that were tangled in her fur.

Once she was all rinsed and clean and it was time to dry off, I lay down next to her in the sun for a cuddle. I couldn't believe how friendly she was. Our bond was instant, honestly it really was. There was the tiniest sparkle in her eyes that gave me some hope we could get her on the mend, despite the grim prognosis from the vet. I'd only met this dog several hours ago, I knew I shouldn't be so drawn into her welfare, but it was too late ... I'd fallen for her.

As her freshly shampooed fur dried in the evening sun, a funny little tuft of hair stuck up. It made me think of the brilliantly spikey wig worn by the American singer Tina Turner in the 1980s. Tina had belted out songs like 'What's Love Got to Do with It' and 'We Don't Need Another

Hero', and had been an absolute queen of rock'n'roll. She didn't just smash record sales, she was the first woman as well as being the first black artist to grace the cover of *Rolling Stone* magazine. She stood out from the crowd. A true trailblazer who also survived domestic abuse at the hands of her husband, Ike. She was a proper icon, and she still is an inspiration to many.

And so in that small moment, this little rescued dog of ours became known as 'Tina Turner'. Another tough cookie, I could tell already, and I hoped this little dog would overcome the bad things life had thrown at her – just like her famous namesake had. 'You're a little superstar too, aren't you?' I grinned at the dog, affectionately ruffling her tufty little head and feeling pleased with the name we'd given her. 'You've got charisma and class, baby.' And I was so pleased to see there was a little twinkle in her eyes.

CHAPTER TWO

WHAT THE HELL IS THE BLOAT?

I'd fallen head over heels in love with Tina from that very moment I'd understood her spirit and named her. But I'm afraid to say that I made a terrible mistake in those first few days. My own inexperience about animal care showed at the worst possible time and it threatened to cost us her life.

By the time Tina had come along I had learned a lot about the basic needs of dogs. I knew the right medications for treating fleas, ticks and worms, the painkillers that were helpful, and how to attend to simple injuries and wounds. I'd spoken to many vets and nutritionists to get educated on the right foods they could be fed, and I'd witnessed first-hand how that made such a big difference to improving their health while not costing the earth.

But I was still a novice really.

Obviously, Tina was massively underweight, so the very first part of her treatment, I confidently assumed, would be to boost the dog up with some decent fresh food. The idea was to get her strong and healthy again after all that time she'd been shackled and malnourished in the dingy basement.

Some rich nutrients inside her, I reasoned, would at least make her dark eyes less sad in the short term. And I knew from the experience I'd had with other dogs that a better diet would soon start improving her poor, mangy skin and fur which would make her more comfortable.

One of her first meals with me, I decided, should be fit for the queen Tina was. So I gave her a large portion of what I thought was a perfect calorie-dense meal – vegetables and meat, something that would nourish her from the inside – which she gratefully gobbled down, as any starving animal would.

But that turned out to be the very worst thing I could have done. My God – the *bloating*. I think back to this now and cringe that I had been so stupid. I just had no idea what the hell it was and hadn't come across it before.

There is this so-called 're-feeding syndrome' which is a super-serious condition. It occurs when too much food has been introduced too quickly to a person or an animal who has been severely malnourished, causing a dangerous shift in fluids and electrolytes which results in a severe case of bloating – it's every bit as uncomfortable for the animal as you'd imagine. It can cause death in humans and it's equally dangerous for dogs, too. But at that time I'd never heard of it.

About ten to fifteen minutes after Tina had happily wolfed down her first dinner, her little stomach swelled up like a balloon, transforming her from a skinny, stick-thin dog into something resembling a hot-air balloon with four limbs sticking out. It was very alarming, to say the least. 'Oh my God, what the hell is happening?' I said in a panic. I ran back to the office where Valeria, who normally helps me out with the animals, was sorting out some paperwork. Luckily for me she was still there and I wasn't alone in this by now very alarming situation.

On top of everything else it was the middle of the night when the vets were all closed. It was just the two of us wondering what the hell we should do at this late hour. Valeria had some basic animal care training, and she recognised the symptoms of 'the bloat' and knew that we were in serious trouble. *Shit.*

I quickly googled what was happening. I was terrified we had killed Tina and I frantically scrolled the internet in search of answers, and found this on one website:

'Bloat develops without warning and can progress quickly. It is always a medical emergency and one of the most rapidly life-threatening conditions that vets treat in dogs. It involves the stomach but can quickly lead to life-threatening shock if left untreated.'

I could feel my blood pressure rapidly going through the roof as I carried on reading …

'When bloat happens, the stomach fills with gas and often twists in a way that it cuts off the blood supply to the gut and stops gas and food from leaving. It can also make the spleen twist and lose circulation, and block vital veins in the back that transport blood to the heart.

'*Bloat is immensely painful for dogs and it can kill in a matter of hours without veterinary intervention.*'

Shit. Shit.

Valeria, luckily, had more experience than me in this area, and she already knew how essential it was that we try and release the build-up of gas in Tina's stomach. And that release would have to come from a needle – literally like physically popping a party balloon. The very idea of this terrified me frankly, but in order to try and save her life it had to be attempted. We both exchanged a serious glance; this wasn't good and neither of us were vets.

Valeria kept her cool – I felt so grateful she was there with us at that moment – and with a look of concentration she managed to carefully locate the right part of the dog's anatomy and insert a small, sharp needle into Tina's stomach. Again I felt so grateful that we had been keeping some basic medical supplies to hand in times of emergencies. For this was surely that.

I soothed Tina as best as I could. She was naturally frightened and had little idea what was going on. 'We're just trying to make you feel better, Tina,' I said, sounding more certain than I felt.

Yet once Valeria had successfully got the needle into poor Tina's awfully swollen belly, the hissing noise that came out of the dog's belly puncture was like a pressure cooker releasing steam. *Yes!*

The relief on both our faces was palpable as we saw her stomach deflate in front of our eyes. It was like something you'd see in a cartoon. I truly thought we had lost her for a moment. But then Tina, under her sparse, thin fur, became as white as a ghost, sweating and slipping in and out of consciousness, fighting for her life. The bloat seemed to have been taken care of, but we were not at all confident this meant she was quite out of the woods yet. I wondered if the drama and this very close call would all prove too much for her little body.

We managed to more or less stabilise her. 'It's late, you should go home, Valeria. Get some rest and I'll see you tomorrow morning,' I said wearily more in hope than anything else. I knew I was far too wound up from the emergency and what a narrow escape it had been to actually sleep that evening. But there was no point for the two of us to keep watch.

I stayed up with Tina all night, feeling absolutely wretched that I'd caused this to happen. As much as I'd learned about dog care, and for all my best intentions, there was clearly still a heck of a lot that – without any veterinary training or science degree – I didn't know.

Nothing in my previous life, either as a young chef or a media guy, had prepared me for this sort of veterinary crisis. I was out of my depth, and I knew it. As soon as Valeria gave me the most tentative thumbs-up I have ever seen, I resolved to do everything to nurse Tina back to health. Sitting next to her that night, I couldn't keep my eyes off her. Every movement, with every small, shallow rise and fall of her tiny belly, I began to think about the kind of life I was sure to give her. If she made it to the morning, I vowed to get better and be better in everything I do for these dogs. I wondered if she was angry with me for putting her in this situation. In that silent, deep night something moved, and as I briefly took my eyes off her to see what it was, I felt alive. Not finding the source of the sound, I quickly turned back to my new companion as she lay on my floor. I suddenly panicked, I couldn't see her breathing. No rise, no fall. It felt like minutes but was most likely seconds, until I saw her take her slow breaths in, and saw the most unexpected thing, her paw, stretched out, twitching and flicking intermittently. I don't know if she was dreaming, I imagined she was, but I knew she was fast asleep. She's safe was all I could let out from under the breath I was holding in. It felt glorious. Everything was alright in the world in that moment.

I knew we desperately needed to feed the poor girl up, but had to take it really slowly. Tina's little body was in such shock that she continued to balloon up, even without food, over the next ten days or so as her system struggled to adjust to this new form of nourishment and care it was suddenly receiving. Those first nights were traumatic wondering from one minute to the next if she was going to be OK. I have to admit I was nervous for both her and me.

I decided that this one needed that extra level of personal care. So I kept her in my own apartment while my guilt would not let up about what had happened to her with the bloat. I had to give her everything I could, and more. The bloat was the last thing this poor girl needed. She seemed utterly exhausted most of the time, and slept through most of it, teetering between life and death.

I really did relate to that feeling of utter tiredness that I saw in Tina, when life circumstances have left you shattered and battered but grimly plugging away. And none of this was Tina's fault; it wasn't fair that her health was suffering now. I couldn't help but wonder about the time some two years earlier when I had been lying at death's door myself, on an intensive care unit ward in a hospital, and how it was in stark contrast to Tina's situation. I was painfully aware that, unlike poor Tina, I had brought on my own close encounter with the grim reaper, all by myself. But that was then.

I'd climb into bed after a long day with the other dogs, and Tina would be curled up there, fragile but warm. She slept in my bed most of the time in those very early days. I'd give her a cuddle and tell her that I had got through this – and I promised that she could too. I just so longed that this would turn out to be true.

CHAPTER THREE

MY OWN ROAD TO RECOVERY

I was an alcoholic when I first arrived in Thailand. I was in a real mess, but alcoholism doesn't appear overnight – and there's rarely any one cause, something I've learned from reading many, many books about other addicts over the years.

I'd grown up as a single child in a middle-class, expat suburb of Brussels, where my father had worked for the European Union (EU). My parents had met as teenagers in Northern Ireland. And by the time I was born in 1979, against the backdrop of 'The Troubles' still rumbling on in their warring homeland, Mum and Dad decided a move to Belgium would provide a better life to raise a family.

I had a lovely, cosy childhood, idyllic even, in those early years. But when I was 13 my mum and dad's marriage hit the rocks. I don't really recall there being many rows, but I'll never forget the hideous event when she walked out on us. As an adult now, I really do understand that she had her reasons, and she's a brilliant, loving mum and we get on great today, I'm pleased to say. But it was confusing as hell at the time, especially because she fell into an abusive relationship with a man I loathed. And I hated myself for not protecting her. I'm not trying to make excuses for why I became a rebellious teenager, but I can see now that I was quite troubled as an adolescent. And in my opinion that made me quite a dysfunctional young adult to be honest. For years, drinking became my way of blotting out the things that hurt inside.

I imagine that's how it begins for a lot of us. You're running away from something that caused pain. And instead of talking about it, you try and cheer yourself up in the short term.

After I was asked to leave a couple of my schools, I didn't end up with any real qualifications. Nor did I know what to do with my life. But I fell in love with reading about food and realised that preparing it – chopping, stirring and creating new dishes – calmed down my busy mind. (I've never been diagnosed with ADHD but I imagine I probably have it or something close to it.)

So I trained as a chef, and quite quickly in my career I got over-promoted to the role of head chef at a prestigious restaurant in Dublin. It was a high-pressure job and I felt horribly out of my depth. I wasn't experienced at management, and I was therefore quite bad at it, and I realised that myself, which then made me worried that everyone hated me. I had crippling anxiety, depression and such severe panic attacks I was convinced my heart was exploding. Several times I even ended up in hospital, so convinced was

I that I was dying. People didn't really discuss mental health back then in the same way they do now. I had no idea what 'panic attacks' really were, or that they can be so severe and flooded with adrenaline it's as if your entire body is being taken over.

We're much more aware of mental health these days, which is real progress. I think the more of us who admit to suffering from it the better, because it then becomes less of a taboo for others to open up about it. And once you talk about it honestly, you can start to get the help you need as well as arm yourself with some useful tools and tricks. But back then, my main way of dealing with the pressures – actually my only way – was to hit the booze. Frequently and heavily.

I ended up changing careers and instead launched a new business with my oldest best friend Sean. We even made it onto the hit BBC show *Dragons' Den* together. But when that venture failed we sadly didn't speak for years. Again, I managed to change track and got into media and advertising where again I was lucky enough to have some success. Yet throughout all these years of my adult life, drinking remained my crutch for decades, destroying my mental health and every relationship I ever had with a woman. I ended up causing them a lot of hurt all the while I was on my road to self-destruction.

So to cut a long story short, by the time I'd sold up the media businesses and had moved to Koh Samui in 2018, I was not in the best shape when it came to my mental health. Or physical, obviously. Thank God I had Snoop, my wonderful rescue dog, who stuck by me as a calming presence throughout all the terrible ups and downs through the years. I've often said that I genuinely might not still be here if it hadn't been for that loyal dog, quietly supporting me and showing me his love as I went on benders followed by miserable comedowns.

When I was at my very lowest ebb and drinking myself to death, at the end of 2020, in any 24-hour window I'd consume (brace yourself) ten cans of beer, four bottles of red wine and a bottle of Thai whisky. I was also a heavy smoker, puffing away on 40-odd Camel Lights a day, and relying on Valium and Xanax to get through the day. (Unlike at home in Europe, where these drugs are prescription-only, in Thailand things are more 'relaxed', and these powerful, addictive medicines are all too easy to buy over the counter.)

I would wake up in my apartment – strewn with empty bottles and pill packets, crushed cans and overfilled ashtrays – with a thumping headache and heart pounding from anxiety. I would be desperately ashamed of the cries for help I'd post on social media when steaming drunk, causing everyone back home a lot of worry. Then I'd hide my phone rather than taking calls or replying to messages, and I'd just go out for more whisky. I spent Christmas Day that year alone, drinking, crying and feeling full of self-loathing.

I wanted life to stop, to end it all with booze and pills, and fall asleep and just … never wake up. Drunkenly, I tweeted words to that effect on 30 December and within a few minutes an ex-girlfriend, one I hadn't spoken to in years, rang me. I picked up the call.

She kept me on the phone for over two hours that night, talking me down from the edge. We chatted about dogs, the weather, silly things really. But it was enough to distract me. Knowing someone cared made me realise I needed urgent medical help. It was like I'd come to the end of the road and her call had, thank God, saved me.

I had reached what is known in rehabilitation terms as my 'rock bottom' and the next day I called my good friend Moritz and begged him to come and get me. I finally checked myself into a hospital on New Year's Eve 2020. As I lay in that hospital bed hooked up to drips, I vowed that if I made it, I *had* to make my life matter.

And it's my work with the street dogs that is the one thing that's really given me purpose and kept me on the straight and narrow.

They're mangy, hungry and unloved – yet I quickly discovered how incredibly cheerful, resilient and joyful they are. It was spending time with them in those early days of my recovery when they taught me so much about how to live, and how just to be present in the moment.

Spending my days in the company of dogs, who are so loving and non-judgemental, changed my world.

In the same month that Tina came into my life, Hope, a very special rescue dog, was finally getting the happy ending she so richly deserved. Sure, she was leaving my life, and that felt strange, but when a kind woman in England volunteered to adopt her I knew it was a positive change in Hope's fortunes. With this line of work, you fall in love with animals all the time, but you simply cannot keep them all – that's not the aim. The goal has to be to give them better lives, whether it's keeping them fed and healthy on the streets where they've come from, or re-homing them with the perfect family for them. Of course I got terribly attached to Hope, as I have to so many, but I always have the bigger picture in my mind: I want to save *thousands*, and *tens of thousands*, of animals. Simply adopting them all would stop that progress dead in its tracks.

I could pluck 500 dogs off the street and put them in a sanctuary tomorrow, but it wouldn't really solve the wider problem. So what we try to do is to sort of help the really sick dogs, whether they might have cancer, or they might have a broken leg, or have been in some kind of traffic accident (the driving here is a little wild let's say). But if we can, we try and fix the dogs on the streets rather than bringing them into the sanctuary. We take them the medicines they need on the streets, we take them off for sterilising procedures to break the cycle of multiplying unwanted animals and we get them vaccinated to protect them from getting sick down the line.

But when they really need it, the sanctuary – now known as Happy Doggo Land – is a place where they can be taken care of until they're back on their feet.

And Hope was one of the first dogs we ever brought to the land so she will always be very close to my heart. She had been shot with a nail gun and slashed with a knife, can you believe it? She came in as a totally broken dog after being so badly abused. I'd recognised from my own depressive episodes that our Hope had simply lost the will to carry on when we first found her.

Yet with time, patience, care and a lot of love, we'd got Hope to a much healthier and far happier place. She was even rolling over and letting me rub her belly and going for beach walks. Hope became a real example for me of how life doesn't have to carry on being lived in darkness. And when a British volunteer called Steff arrived to help out and ended up falling in love with the dog, she decided she was going to adopt her and give Hope the forever home this dog so richly deserved.

Knowing Hope would be travelling to her forever home that month just made my heart want to burst with joy and pride. It had been a real success story.

People message me all the time on Instagram, saying, 'Oh, just take the dog home with you, Niall.' And I always want to explain why that would just be impossible, however much I wanted to.

I always knew that I was never going to be able to solve the street dog problem by re-homing them, there's simply too many to attempt that. But it's a lovely thing for the individual dogs it happens to when we can find suitable homes.

It's also nice for people who are following their story, and who have been invested in these dogs' journeys, to see them thrive and know they're getting their happy ending. These are just normal dogs after all, who desperately want to be loved.

So it was very cool and very rewarding getting the news that Hope was travelling off to pastures new. And I knew right from the start of meeting Tina that this was the kind of story I wanted for her, too.

CHAPTER FOUR

TINA: MEET NIALL, JUMBO AND SNOOP

My home is a very basic, humble structure. It's a small house just overlooking the land and it is about a two-minute walk from where the doggies come to stay. It is a simple, modest house that's quite common in Thailand and the inside is just as basic as the outside of it. It's very much a minimalist lifestyle and I have absolutely nothing in the house that I don't need. My only possessions here are a laptop to work on in the evenings, my clothes and a few books that I would love to read one day. I don't have a TV, special art on the walls or anything that might be seen as fancy. As long as I have my nice comfortable bed, a shower and place to have one or two sick dogs and clean clothes, that's all I need in life.

It just so happens that when Tina came into my life I was already looking after Snoop and Jumbo. Snoop was my very own dog who followed me from Manchester to my new life in Thailand (more on him later). But Jumbo, boy, oh boy, Jumbo was a one-of-a-kind dog.

He was a big, chunky, chocolate brown labrador type dog who had serious health issues that made his legs balloon so it kind of looked like he had baggy trousers on. He and I were in and out of the vets for two years trying to fix his issues, but it never really affected his quality of life.

Jumbo came to live with me quite simply because I fell in love with his personality and character from the very first moment. He was a big lump of a dog but lived by his own terms, either sleeping or chasing the finer things in life (play, food, friendship). When we'd go for a stroll, it was like, *There go Laurel and Hardy off on their silly walk.* That's how I felt we looked.

Having lived on the streets before he had become my part pet, part street dog, part comedy sidekick, Jumbo was prone to wandering off. In fact, he used to sneak out of my little house and head off down to the local 7-Eleven which was about 200 yards away. He would sit there and beg tourists and passers-by for food as if he was a street dog. He had the look down to a tee and was very successful. I lost count of the times I would have to go down there at 11 p.m., which was my bedtime, and drag him back by the scruff of the collar like a parent getting their kid out of a school disco.

Jumbo also stopped in restaurants, cafés and even a little pub where everybody knew him and would give him a few treats. Daytimes would be reserved for sleeping off the previous day's activities like a sort of doggy hangover before he'd go and do it all again.

I just wish everyone had got the chance to meet this gentle goofball.

Tina had fitted in beautifully at home with Snoop and Jumbo. Snoop and Jumbo were firm friends but the introduction of Tina, the lady, slightly worried me. It need not have done as both dogs turned out to be total gentlemen, who instinctively seemed to understand that this poorly newcomer, Tina, was frail and needed our love. They weren't threatened by this interloper one tiny bit. And they instantly warmed to her kind soul. It was obvious to everyone who came across Tina – humans *and* other dogs – that here was a golden retriever with the sweetest nature, and it would have been impossible for any dog to have ever taken against her. There was no snarling or threat. Tina's inherent goodness simply shone through and charmed everyone.

The first week I had her in the apartment with us was a blur of worry, hope and small victories. I spent most of my time nursing her, determined to keep her alive. And slowly, after a couple of weeks or so, once the terrifying bloat incidents had stopped, she started to show signs of improvement. She went on short walks, including her first ever little beach walk (always a highlight of any day here) and she began showing more energy each day.

She was bright and had started to give me her paw, offering a little wag of her tail in a show of her canine appreciation. Her chances of surviving might only have been 50–50, but I am always an optimist and had decided in my mind she was going to make it.

And I really wanted Tina to know that not all humans were bad. She obviously was a special dog for holding onto life as long as she had, and I was taking care of her now to make up for that.

I'm not sure whether I twigged this at the time, but there was something about Tina that brought back more of my unhappy and slightly complicated childhood memories. I guess her being a mummy of all the pups that she'd been separated from, most likely before it was time to do so, triggered those memories again. I didn't even realise I'd tried to blot them out from all that time ago, but I was suddenly transported back to the moment when I woke up in my family home to find that my mum had left us. The day before she was there when I got back from school, and the next day she was no longer there. It's still one of the most isolating feelings I have ever experienced, that hurt and confusion, and trying to understand what causes this bewilderment has made me question so many things throughout my life. I think we all just want to belong somewhere and have someone to care and be loved by.

That may sound silly comparing my own life to dogs, but that's what I do all the time, to be honest. And another observation I've had many times over since I started all this is how dogs are so much purer and kinder souls than us humans. Whereas I distrusted people for years and pushed women away as an adult – for fear of ever being rejected and hurt again I suppose – animals seemed more forgiving and trusting than I used to be.

Tina had every right to be wary of any human, but instead she immediately opened her heart to me and gave me her total trust. She clung to me those nights in that first week or two, trying to get as close as possible, even curling up right on my head some nights as if seeking comfort and safety. Admittedly, when it happened at four in the morning I wasn't *always* loving this attention … but I certainly marvelled at this instinct given that this retriever had never experienced kind human contact before. The pair of us misfits had bonded so deeply, and I quickly became incredibly protective of her.

I had a gut instinct about this dog, it was like meeting an old friend or, without meaning to sound too 'woo woo', some soul from a past life. I loved every bone in that skinny little body and I refused to write her off.

We ferried her to various vets to try and get a grip on her health, and it was diagnosed that she had broken ribs at some stage that needed to be assessed as they hadn't mended in the way they should. The stomach complications she had from being so malnourished needed fixing, while the skin problems could probably be treated in the longer term.

Tina's appetite returned, though I had to carefully manage her portions to avoid another terrifying episode of re-feeding syndrome. She drank water constantly and was on medication, absorbing as much of life as she could. It became really clear to everyone that she wanted to live.

The vets were cautiously optimistic, saying if we could get her through the first phase and bulk her up a bit, she had a chance. Severe malnutrition was her biggest issue, but there was hope.

By the time Tina had been in our lives for several weeks, she'd gone from weighing just 12.5 kg (25 lb), and essentially looking at death's door, to weighing a far less frail 21 kg (43 lb). She'd also, happily, started actually looking like the gloriously yellow-furred golden retriever she was, as she grew bigger and stronger by the day.

And the more I shared about Tina the more people fell for her. She just looked so adorable in her little bandanas. People often ask me why I get the dogs wearing bandanas, the little scraps of brightly coloured cotton I tie around the dogs' necks, like a bohemian-looking kind of collar I suppose. It's become a sort of 'signature' statement or whatever they call it in the fashion world.

The whole idea of using these bandanas really started when I just had a few of them lying around my flat. Some people use them to protect their head from the beating sun out here. Personally, I love a hat, it's just practical and safe when you live in a hot country and spend a lot of the day working outside. But for some reason I had some of these funny bandanas, cheap and cheerful things, lying around.

At first, I picked one up thinking they would look cute on the dogs. I can't remember now which rescue dog was given the first one, but as time went on I realised there was more to it than just cuteness. These bandanas actually gave the street dogs a sense of belonging. I mean, think about it, here are these dogs, living on the streets, with nothing to their name. They've been abandoned, forgotten, and left to fend for themselves. I realise that there were two things I could give them that cost nothing at all but made a difference somehow – a bandana and a name. Of course, it's the medicine, food and vet care that are the big essentials, but I decided there was something really powerful about giving them an *identity*, as well as some love and affection.

And the simple act of tying a bandana around their necks and giving them a name seemed to resonate with people and make them smile. God knows there are enough downers in this line of work, and in life in general some days. Why *not* do the little things that give you a bit of a lift on a day when life feels like an uphill struggle?

When I walk away, and see the dogs wearing them from a distance, proudly sporting their little bright materials around their necks, I catch myself thinking, *Don't they look nice?* They've got a name, and they look like they're ready to face the day. Now, I don't know how much it means to the dogs themselves, but I like to think that when they have their little bandanas on, they feel a bit smarter, a bit more put-together and maybe even a bit more loved.

That's how it all started really, but people had noticed them, including Zoe, a girl who came to Koh Samui to volunteer with us for a bit. She was super-creative and asked if she could do something special for the dogs. 'Go for it!' I said, of course.

In Thailand, you find all these wonderfully skilled Indian and Nepalese tailors who can make just about anything. Some people return home from a holiday in Thailand with a suitcase of new clothes, taking advantage of the skills out here and good value prices.

So, lovely Zoe went out and bought some fabrics, and custom-designed special bandanas for Tina – one for each day of the week. I was so delighted – it's the small, sweetest and thoughtful things that really make my day.

Tina had a bandana for every occasion: a glamorous Friday night bandana with little baubles on it, a sporty one and even a cosy pyjama-style one for chilling out. She wore a different one every day; they became her thing. Tina looked so elegant in them, and for a dog that was initially so broken it was a boost to everyone's spirits to see her now have pride in herself. The bandanas really symbolised just how far she'd come and how her dignity had been restored after years spent having to sleep and eat in those horrific conditions we found her in.

CHAPTER FIVE

BUSTER'S STORY

Around two months after we'd rescued her, Tina was in a much better place physically and properly looked like a golden retriever. Her fur had mostly grown back by now and the weight she so badly needed to put on had been slowly and, thank God, safely gained. No more bloat for this girl.

And she'd made a little pal with a newcomer to the land who we named Buster. Dogs, like humans, come in all different shapes and sizes. And we can't all be little cuties to look at. Buster was one of those animals who, rightly or wrongly, you might take one look at and decide you don't want to get very close to. But whoever was scared of Buster the dog was arguably nowhere near as terrified as Buster himself after he'd spent a long time on a short chain.

His story, like Tina and so many other dogs, began with a photo appearing on my phone. Not from a tourist this time, but a concerned local who had noticed things were not right.

I squinted at the screen trying to see what the problem was. It looked like a pitbull terrier. The sort of dog people

TINA

can be a bit scared of, the kind who might be wearing a muzzle in the UK, or one of those that flash up on the TV on the news when there's a story of a dangerous dog committing an attack.

He was a dark sandy colour with big round paws and you could see from his frame that he was meant to be solid and heavily muscled like pitbulls classically are. But this dog had been chained up on an incredibly short leash, only about the length of your arm, and he looked pretty sorry for himself on the hard concrete. On the evidence of that picture we received, he certainly wasn't out terrorising the locals like a stereotypical pitbull; it seemed more like the animal was the one who was terrified.

We'd been told that this dog had an owner, and were provided with their address. It was time to be reunited with my old trusted firend Rod and off we headed down there to see what was going on. I instinctively sensed that this situation was going to require a bit of tact and diplomacy. Rod and I gently knocked on the door of the person we had been told owned this dog, along with a nice local who sometimes kindly came along to act as our Thai translator and who introduced us to the owner, and explained that we helped dogs and were interested in learning more about this dog's situation. Immediately on the defensive, the owner said that this was an 'extremely aggressive dog', and that it was very 'dangerous'. That's why they had him on a chain they said. A short chain that

56

was quite inhumane. This was all the owner was really saying, stressing to us over and over again that this dog was considered very, very dangerous locally.

Obviously, I listened. I love dogs but I don't have a death wish. I wouldn't abandon efforts to help the animal, but I didn't want to be savagely attacked in the process.

Gingerly, I leaned in to have a closer look at this animal. I could see that his tail was covered with horrible-looking growths that looked a bit like human warts. We tried discreetly talking to other locals, being mindful to be out of earshot of the owner, to try and ask them about what they thought might have been going on here. Trying to build up a picture is part of understanding what may have happened and knowing what the best course of action to take might be.

The general consensus was that this unfortunate dog had been confined on a short chain to this small area of cement. The tropical Thai rains make cement really damp and the standing pools of rainwater can get pretty stagnant and mucky. So the poor thing had been living and sleeping in this unsanitary area in a mix of mucky water and unshaded sun. A group of neighbours had noticed him and were worried, and one of them had then been the one to pluck up the courage to report it to us.

The concerned neighbour told us that they had been sneaking the dog water. They seemed to think that the owner wasn't giving him anything to eat or drink – and hadn't been for a while. Can you imagine that? All in all, here was a pretty sorry-looking dog. And it seemed worse, and more starkly *wrong* in some ways, to see in front of us a breed that we usually associate with power and assertiveness looking so rough. So pathetically sad.

I tried to put the emotions that this was stirring in me aside and adopted a practical, cool-headed approach. How I saw it was that we had two issues to face: a) how to approach the dog and b) how to handle the owner. *Should be fairly straightforward, huh Niall?*

I decided I'd have a go at befriending the dog. What do dogs love? Food and balls, of course. And that's how I found myself cradling a can of wet food under one arm and holding a tennis ball in the other, walking slowly like I was in some kind of cowboy film. Small careful steps forward. From what I'd heard and seen from this distance, this wasn't going to be easy. Nothing ever is, is it? Tiny beads of sweat began to form under my floppy hat, and I really should have drunk more water; the heat was insanely intense, beating down on me, wearing me down step by step.

'This dog is going to bite your arm off ...' said a voice, followed by a muted '... you Western idiot.' I looked to the side and saw the stern owner standing there, hands on his hips sucking his teeth and muttering his warning. I thought to heed his advice but carried on – after all the animal genuinely seemed friendly enough. So I carried on. Slowly. Very slowly. And just as I got closer to the dog, the owner started shouting at the top of his voice from a safe distance, which didn't go unnoticed, 'Wow! That's insane! People can't get anywhere near him!' I didn't think it was that bad, but this guy was really laying it on.

'Don't be fooled,' he said, 'nobody gets this close. He's going to go for you when you get close enough.'

I am not going to lie, by this stage I was pretty terrified as I inched closer, waving the ball and showing the dog the food like some kind of zookeeper in the tiger enclosure. I was genuinely waiting for him to go for me ... but he didn't, and he remained pretty chilled.

It was hard to work out what was going on. But eventually, we got him into a dog box and started to work on the owner. We told him the dog clearly needed medical attention and we could take him to a vet so he could be looked over. The owner was very resistant and kept saying, 'The dog stays here' (making violent and slightly alarming hand movements to emphasise 'here'). As we pointed out all the medical issues this poor dog had, first the wart-like growths on the tail, then other scabs which looked infected, then showing how his breathing was fast and shallow, the guy eventually changed his mind and allowed us to take the dog. I don't know if the owner was feeling bad by this point, but he certainly didn't show it and was still telling us how aggressive this dog could be.

As I finally took the dog away I wasn't sure whether I was more relieved to be shot of the owner, or to finally have the dog in my care. The first stop was the vet's surgery, so once in the car we stepped on it! I wanted to see what we were dealing with. And there, they diagnosed a few things. Firstly, there was a nasty fungal infection, which probably wasn't just in his skin but throughout poor Buster's whole body. The kind of infection that humans only get if their immune system is extremely suppressed, and they can be dangerous. He also had something wrong with his lungs, which was mostly because he'd been forced to become so unfit by being chained. This could probably be improved with some general rehabilitation.

We'd also noticed there was swelling – a blood clot in his ear – something the vets call aural haematomas, which are quite common in dogs with floppy ears. Often, you can just put a little hole into the area and the congealed blood will slowly liquify and drain out. But here it seemed like the blood had really clotted hard in his ear. The vet tried all sorts – special bandages, antibiotics, anti-inflammatories – but it must have been there for so long and he'd been so badly neglected, that the only option the vet had was to amputate his ear.

Buster already looked scary, like a street sort of pitbull who would be mean in a fight – so with a missing ear too, well, he wasn't ever going to have the appearance of a cuddly teddy bear.

Everyone was still handling him very carefully at this time because of this apparent mean streak he had, and when we brought him to the land to recover, we were very careful with how we settled him into his kennel. We couldn't have him attacking the other dogs or attacking us humans.

But as his medical conditions improved, it seemed that he actually wasn't a 'bad' dog at all in terms of temperament. What quickly transpired was that Buster was one of the biggest softy goofballs we'd ever come across – and he became a real favourite. We realised that he was definitely a sandwich short of a picnic, he could never really learn any tricks or that kind of thing, but he was such a loving and caring dog. As we found new dogs to look after, we started to put those who were the most vulnerable, or the most scared, in with Buster because he'd make such an effort to look after them, and he'd never argue or fight.

It was sweet and very funny because I'd have him in with maybe two or three new puppies and I would bring in three bowls of food. The cheeky puppies would go over and steal Buster's food, and while any other big dog would probably have growled to scare them off, this dopey big pitbull would just walk away with his shoulders slumped down and be like, 'Oh, I guess I just lost my food!'

I don't think the poor guy had been off that short chain for years so you could tell he was itching to explore. Hilariously, the first thing he did was to go straight over and start sniffing the flowers. I will always remember that here was this tough-looking dog who people would probably cross the street to avoid, and who couldn't really walk more than 10 or 20 yards at the start because of breathlessness, and here he was trundling over to smell the flowers.

I used to watch him and think it was a bit like a patient walking round the hospital grounds, trying to get better. And with this little exercise regime Buster did slowly start to improve. As well as smelling the flowers, he loved to paddle around with Tina and the others on the beach. As they did doggy paddle in the water they looked so cute, and the sight of funny old one-eared Buster in there with them, as if he'd just escaped from a street fight, was quite the picture.

Tina brought out the best in Buster. Both of them had once been on short chains but Tina showed Buster a way out, a new life. Tina seemed like she was on top of the world and loving life, and maybe he too could be there one day.

CHAPTER SIX

STERILISING AND SOCIAL MEDIA

Spring was fast approaching and Tina had long settled in and had really seemed to be thriving. She was well enough, we decided, to have a sterilisation operation. It was especially important to have that taken care of now that she was out and about having fun and socialising with other dogs on our walks.

Tina had spent so many unhappy years being used for breeding puppies, which had completely worn out her body, getting the operation was particularly symbolic and a start of a better future ahead. I felt incredibly proud of her as I got her ready to be sent off to the vets, like we did with all the others. It was hard to know exactly how old she was, to tell you the truth, but the vet guessed around eight, which meant she could still technically get pregnant, and that was the very last thing Tina needed – or any of us for that matter.

It might seem like a small footnote in the bigger scheme of things for Tina, but it still felt like a significant moment of closure for this wonderful lady.

'Don't you worry, angel,' I kissed her affectionately on her wet snout before she went under the general anaesthetic. 'We're just making sure you never have to have another puppy in your life again.'

Not only would her ill health not have coped with a pregnancy, but I felt she deserved to just focus on being a dog for the first time in her life, and sharing all the amazing love and affection she had to give.

To be very precise Tina was the 521st dog we have sterilised since starting this mission to solve the street dog problems in Thailand. And yes, I really do keep count of each and every one, as it just means so much to me. I used to keep a count in my head but now I've developed a helpful spreadsheet. I know their little quirks, like who doesn't like the rain, or who needs their skin checked during the wet season. When a dog is walking a little gingerly, I can look at them and know if it's serious or not. If they are a little underweight or need to see a vet. I don't have kids but I guess this is a similar way parents would know through intuition about their kids. With 80 dogs to look after, I know the odds are stacked against me in terms of keeping them all healthy and alive, but they are my pride and joy. I think of it as having 80 pets that happen to live on the streets.

But the first dog I ever got neutered was Mr Fox, one of the kindest and most fun dogs I've ever met. His name fit him perfectly as his big bushy tail could swirl up at around 100 miles an hour when I arrived on the moped with the food.

On the day of the big chop, I'm not sure who was more anxious going to the vets in the jeep that day. Mr Fox was about to lose his precious body parts but I was beyond nervous that I would somehow end up getting it wrong. I mean I wasn't performing the surgery myself, obviously, but I felt a great deal of responsibility for this cheeky scamp that had whirled into my life with his hairy helicopter tail. I think deep down the root of my worry was that maybe, despite all the will, I was not cut out to help the dogs.

After catching him in a hastily purchased crate, luring him in with food and proudly transporting him to the vets in my recently acquired second-hand jeep, I successfully had him 'done'. And he was marked with a little 'V' tattoo in his ear, as a sign to anyone else trying to neuter dogs that this one had been taken care of in that department. After it had all gone smoothly I then put him safely back where he lived in the jungle. I made sure he got the necessary medications to ward off infections, and it was so satisfying to know he would not be out there sowing his wild oats and creating any more little Mr or Miss Foxes.

The last I saw of Mr Fox was him bounding around in the snow in the glorious mountains of Montana, USA with his new family, so it's fair to say his surgery went without a hitch. I'll always remember that first time with Mr Fox because it felt like a real turning point. He was a dog from the jungle and a gentle soul, but if this was going to work and my mission was going to succeed, we needed to deal directly with the problem.

For the next six to eight months, I was doing all the catching and ferrying to the vets alone. And it was hard work. I got bitten three times and crawled under many shacks and ran up hills and into rivers trying to get those dogs. I only managed to do 302 sterilisations in those first eight months as I had to drive two per day to the vets myself. But I wanted to understand the problems and catch the dogs myself so I could work out how to do it more efficiently.

That experience was absolutely crucial in forming my understanding of how hard it is, but also how important this was for the dogs. In my local area I could quickly see the small difference it was making. It was a lightbulb moment in my head. This was how you improved not just a few dozen lives, but thousands.

Only eight months later, I made a big decision which would change things significantly. I decided I would focus on raising money and awareness of my work to accelerate sterilising targets both on Koh Samui and around the world. In order to achieve our sterilising targets we required partners urgently, who we'd need to fund at scale and get the whole programme turbo boosted. It became the perfect example of how you can do a little bit on your own, but when people pull together as part of a team we can all achieve so much more.

A year on from fixing the delightful Mr Fox, we did a further 1,500 procedures. Each dog we do costs about $50 so it's quite a lot of money, and it's quite a lot of logistics. Sometimes you need to carefully sedate the aggressive dogs (and yes, I've been bitten by dogs who weren't quite as out for the count as I'd thought), but it's the only way to stem the rise in street dogs and get the numbers down.

Anything else, as I frequently say, is just sticking a Band-Aid on a gaping wound.

I think there's 500 million street dogs in the world – that's more than the population of America – and I want to halve that in my lifetime. Sounds crazy, but I think I can do it, and I'm really proud of the fact that we now have eight other partners in three countries, not just Thailand but Sri Lanka and Indonesia, too.

Until as recently as 2022, I wasn't even aware of what neutering was. In the space of just two and half years, we have amazingly reached 90 to 95 per cent coverage of dogs sterilised here on the island of Koh Samui. We can never get to having 100 per cent of the dogs sterilised in any given area because some locals won't allow their dogs to be done; there are still, sadly, some dog breeders who want to make money from puppies, and dogs are still being brought in by workers. But we've stopped a vast amount of unwanted, unloved and uncared lives being brought into this world.

I'm also incredibly proud, to be honest, of our more practical and mundane work behind the scenes. While the work isn't as fun as feeding a greedy bunch of street dogs, these ops are absolutely essential in that they change lives. But let's be honest, they're not always the most gripping things to report on. But the good news is that as you read this we have sterilised 70,000 dogs. It might sound like a large and slightly abstract number but that is actually 70,000 operations. It is and has been an expensive mission but in my estimations it has stopped up to a million puppies being born unwanted.

When Tina came back from her own sterilising op, a little groggy but perfectly safe, it really felt like a fresh start. This was her second chance at life and I felt that she so deserved it. I could feel something different in the air. Something had shifted, and I was sure this was the new start we needed for an old girl.

And by that time, Tina had won the hearts of literally everyone she came across – from the veterinary staff who cooed over her, and the postman who brought her treats, to every single volunteer who helped care for her. She was loving, affectionate and so clearly thankful to be alive. We all couldn't wait to see her every day and have her joy in life rub off on us, too.

People seemed to adore the fact that she'd come so far from being the gangly poor mite with sores and bald patches, who could barely remember how to use her own legs, and – in front of all of our eyes – she had transformed into an animal full of beans, with wolfy big grins for anyone who paid her attention, and who could forget her deliciously enchanting waggy tail.

She enjoyed running on the beach, fetching tennis balls and giving me her paw. She got on well with all the other dogs, but it was always humans Tina liked best, and she constantly sought out our company.

For every story I shared of Tina, whether it's her walking around the land with that happy look on her face or her lying down to escape the heat of the day, I got about 20 times more messages and 'likes' on social media than any other dogs. Some animals seem to especially capture people's imagination. I still can't really get my head around how popular our mission has been and how many people it has reached. Tina encapsulated the best in all of us and brought us all closer together.

In the beginning, I started sharing my daily interactions with random, sometimes cheeky, sometimes greedy, sometimes downright comic street dogs, with a few friends. Fast forward to today and it's an online community of like-minded, dog-loving people who care deeply about the dogs and their respective journeys.

I've completely lost track of my messages, which feels worrying in all honesty, as I hate to think people believe I'm ignoring them. I used to personally reply to everyone, but I literally would get nothing done if I still did that. But it doesn't mean I wouldn't like to. Or that I don't care. I love that people want to follow the stories of the dogs and I'm so grateful.

But despite our voices being heard, I was still very surprised when I was approached to write my first book about my experiences and my life. I'd never seen myself as a writer and in all honesty I wasn't sure I could do it. Was I ready to share it all? I know I share a lot of it online, but this was different, this was a book. Would anyone be interested? This was going to be in shops and at airports and wherever books are sold, I was told. But how would I do it? I was so busy with the work I was building, I didn't feel I could commit. I was flattered to be asked, of course, but it was something I had to think long and hard about.

Look, I never fall into the trap of thinking I'm anything special. I'm hardly a celebrity. I give every penny I make to the mission and I can't think of anything worse than being famous. I don't need much in life, just shoes on my feet and clothes on my back and enough money to run my moped and eat.

I'm also actually a very shy person at heart, which was probably why I relied on drink for so many messy years. It gave me a false sense of confidence (which I bet is how many people get into an unhealthy relationship with booze). Sure, I might have been the life and soul at parties some nights, and was generally the last man standing in any bar, but I was rarely drinking to have a good time. At least not in the latter days.

It was more to mask a lot of my feelings of inferiority and natural anxiety. And when drink makes you behave in ways you wouldn't when sober, well, when you then wake up and cringe about things it only increases your anxiety and paranoia. Everyone knows this really, and I knew it too. But I was trapped in a cycle. Drinking to feel better. Then ending up feeling a hell of a lot worse. Wretched mainly. And having another drink became the quickest way to fix it. And on and on.

Since I've stopped drinking I've definitely felt more comfortable and at ease with who I really am, and improving the lives of street dogs has given me a purpose in life and a reason to carry on. I needed that.

But getting attention? That's not me at all.

Of course it's fantastic to have more people following the dogs' stories. I try so hard to make sure I'm updating wherever I can all the goings-on around my life. I enjoy writing for our newsletter – it gives me an enormous sense of joy to sit down in the evening and tell people about our day and progress. It's kind of like writing a diary. And I'm really pleased that Happy Doggo now has its own YouTube channel which is aimed at young people; after all educating kids about animal welfare is vital. Changing the attitudes of the next generation will make an enormous difference in this field. And children are natural animal lovers – I've seen that first-hand time and again.

My inbox these days is overflowing with requests, offers to promote dog products and all sorts of intriguing projects. It would be so easy to get swept up in it all, letting the excitement take me in a million different directions, chasing fame or a quick buck.

But here's the thing. I have had to make one strict rule and it guides me every single time I consider doing something. I pause, and ask myself one simple question: *Will this help improve the lives of street dogs?*

If the answer is no, I don't do it. It's as simple as that. Some might wonder how posting a video of an old dog relaxing or having their first bath could possibly help street dogs. But for me, it's all about education and awareness. Sure, I can personally save a few hundred dogs, but with the collective power of thousands of people from all over the world, we can save millions together. I might not always get it right, and sometimes I come under flak, but that's the honest thinking behind everything I do.

To be totally truthful, my own idea of a perfect day would be spent alone in the jungle, feeding dogs and not talking to a single soul. I think I have always been introverted, ever since I was little. What that means is that I just really like my own company. I think it's easy to sometimes see people and think, wow, they're so great at talking to people and being social, but the reality might be so far removed from that.

Most people are inherently social but there are some of us out there who are introverts through and through. I don't need to be around lots of people. Give me a couple of dogs and the closed door of my little house in the evening on my own and I'm a very happy person.

That said, I'm also keenly aware that I've been given an incredible opportunity. I might be reluctant to get my mug out there, especially on days when my mental health is wobbly, but I know I'm also in a unique position to make a real difference for street dogs.

Rest assured that I'm keeping my feet firmly on the ground. I'm 45 now and a grown-up. It's only just begun.

I figure as long as I stay true to my mission, I know I'm on the right path. The recognition, the plaudits – that's all secondary. What really matters is using this opportunity I now have to bring about positive change for the dogs who need it most. And Tina showed me exactly how much that help was needed and what a difference it can make.

CHAPTER SEVEN

LIVING HER
BEST LIFE

With Tina's health seemingly under control, there was no stopping her. Her eyes shone, her mane gleamed and her tail wagged. A lot. *Bring it on.* That was her attitude, as she trotted along full of beans by my side, holding herself high in her jaunty bandanas. And my God, that joy she radiated was so infectious. For someone like me (who can be grumpy and overwhelmed by life at times) she made me

lighten up, take life less seriously and start acting like a kid at Christmas again.

I can still laugh out loud thinking of the pair of us riding around on my scooter together, with Tina next to me on the bike in her makeshift sidecar. I'd got the idea after spotting a local guy driving around on the island with one, and as soon as I saw him, well, I just knew I had to get Tina in one of those. I knew she was going to love it: she embraced any adventure I put in front of her, especially if it meant me being her comedy sidekick.

If you've seen any of the *Wallace and Gromit* films, like the mega-popular *A Close Shave*, you might remember Wallace, the hapless inventor, riding around with Gromit, the much more savvy dog, in a red sidecar. That's exactly how Tina and I felt on the island's pathways.

Experiencing the wind on her fur and the warm sunshine on her back as we whizzed by palm trees under clear blue skies seemed just as heavenly to her as it always has to me. I put my foot down on that pedal and ramped up the speed a bit and it was like seeing a kid squealing with delight asking to be spun harder on the waltzer at a fairground.

I wanted to make sure she was safe of course, so I went into Tesco (yes, the great British supermarket brand has reached Thailand too now) to look for a pair of glasses to protect her eyes from the wind. All I could find were a pink pair of kids' swimming glasses. Oh well, I thought, they'll do the job nicely, and they certainly made me chuckle.

She looked hilarious – and absolutely perfect. Coupled up with a blue helmet, Tina turned into the ultimate style icon riding next to me. Like Penelope Pitstop from the Hanna-Barbera cartoon. It all made me laugh so much I had to remember to focus on the road ahead and not just keep looking at her gleeful expression. I have never in my life seen a dog who was more proud or more happy to be riding in a little sidecar wearing pink goggles. It's not exactly a regular sight though, admittedly, but perhaps it should be?!

There's a child in me that thinks life should be like some sort of art class or games day from when we were kids and didn't have a worry in the world. Life can't just all be about spreadsheets, checking what days the bins go out and counting calories.

Helping the dogs is quite taxing mentally so I always have my head racing with little fun ideas to not only please the dogs but to put a smile on us humans' faces also. I'd seen Tina starting to love tennis balls which was a real delight for me after she had been tied up on the chain for so long. Here was a golden retriever doing what she should have been doing her whole life which was just chasing a ball and bringing it back to her human friend.

Although she was still thin and recovering I could see her face absolutely light up when I brought the ball out. We all see that with our dogs from sticks or mentioning a walk or treat – there is always something that will trigger a burst of pure joy from our dogs. The sight of the tennis ball to Tina was like winning the lottery.

But I am not entirely sure that Tina knew what tennis balls were the first time she saw one – she really liked them, but I did wonder if anyone had ever played with her. As soon as she got the smell and the taste and feel of their squishiness in her mouth, well, she could not leave those round yellow things out of her sight.

Honest to God, she'd walk around all day long with one in her mouth beside me, as if so proud of it and never wanting to let it go. Yes, often they'd be plenty of drool and you'd be throwing it back all wet in your hand as every dog owner knows. But it was a joy to see.

I was driving one Sunday when I thought, 'Imagine if I could get Tina a hundred tennis balls, how happy she would be!' Then I thought about how I could give them to her as a surprise.

That's how after a couple of hours' planning I ended up buying all the supplies to make her dreams come true. A couple of people were helping me that afternoon walk the dogs and they thought I had absolutely lost my mind as I climbed a tree with a hundred tennis balls in a large green washing basket. Tina had been distracted off to one side. I was about ten feet up in the air and one wrong move would have seen me fall and break my back, but I knew this was worth it.

Tina wandered towards the tree and at just the right moment I was able to release the one hundred tennis balls down around her. It must have felt like the greatest day of her life as the skies opened with her favourite things ever. She ran from ball to ball for hours, sniffing and playing with them and bringing them back to me with a look of utter bewilderment mixed with unbridled joy. She kept running around greedily trying to pick up two at a time before moving on to the next one and then the next one. She'd bring them over to me so proudly, dropping them all soggy at my feet, as if desperate to show them to me. *Look, Niall, there's been a tennis ball miracle, isn't it amazing!*

Eventually, after about two hours (yes *two* hours) she lay down among those tennis balls and fell sound asleep. Probably dreaming of them. Exhausted from exhilaration.

All I could think about was how she had been on that chain a few weeks earlier with misery etched on her face ... and now here she was with a dream coming true.

I realised then that it wasn't just the physical tennis balls that she loved. It was the fact that she had someone to share them with. That thought can still make me well up, to be honest.

Some people might look at a little stunt like that and wonder how it helps with my mission to save street dogs. How does spending two hours like that, climbing a tree and creating a fleeting moment for one dog, help end suffering? The answer is that it absolutely does because it brings out the child in me, it makes Tina have a memory she'd never forget and it helps put a smile on many people's faces. In a life that can be so tough with bad news and doom and gloom, we all need moments where the sky reigns with tennis balls to spur us on. When I'm lying on my own deathbed taking my last breaths, I won't be thinking about the new iPhone I once had or the fancy pair of designer shoes (or in my case it's more likely to be a pair of running shoes). I'll be thinking about Tina and her face as she was running from tennis ball to tennis ball.

But the special moments with Tina didn't always involve events or funny things captured on social media; it was in all the small, day-to-day dog chores (of which there are many in this funny old life of mine) when the golden retriever's heart and soul really shone through.

Tina followed me everywhere, she was always within about two feet of wherever I was.

I don't mean that in the way that some dogs do, where you go to the toilet and they are standing outside the door, or staring at you while you eat. (Which is sweet/needy or slightly annoying depending on the person, the animal and the mood.) Her presence felt more gentle, more kind somehow. Like she was watching, supporting and wanting to help with the 'non-fun but essential stuff'.

Every day I do what I call the 'sick rounds', a little bit like a doctor does on a hospital ward, just to check in with the patients (in this case the poorly mutts) and where they are with their recovery (or not, sadly). Tina would be there, right beside me. She would be checking in and gently cleaning little puppies, or just keeping a watchful eye and bringing her own unique calming presence to general proceedings. She might have been parted from all the puppies she had to be forced to breed in her former, miserable life. But that natural motherly instinct was always in her. She loved to give. You know those so-called 'vampire' types of people in our lives whose presence can suck the life out of you? Tina was the very opposite of that: she radiated life in every direction and lifted us all up in every imaginable way.

Like the day we found a teeny tiny puppy – barely the size of my hand – dumped in the jungle. The poor little mite, covered in ticks and fleas, wouldn't have lasted more than 24 hours all alone without a mum. So, of course we took her straight in and started to look after her, feeding her goat's milk for nourishment. But the abandoned pup needed a mum really, and we didn't need to think long about who might best nurture her with some maternal TLC.

Tina had already swung into action to take little Solo (as we named the puppy for obvious reasons) under her wing. The pair of them soon became inseparable and Solo worshipped the ground that Tina walked on. Like a real

daughter, Solo even started to pick up Tina's little manner-isms and her gentle, kind ways. Tina was always fussing over Solo and sharing her toys, making sure the pup felt cared for. It was beautiful to watch.

Under the influence of her foster mummy, Solo became the gentlest, sweetest little angel, and I'm thrilled to say that there was a happy ending for Solo – my own little brother Ruadh fell in love with her after my family had visited. After begging our dad for several months, we found a forever home for Solo who is now living her best life in Belgium. Tina would be so proud.

As well as her caring nature, Tina also had a natural authority about her, without ever flexing her muscles or barking about it. Dogs naturally fall out, of course: they can get macho or bristle or snap at each other when annoyed, just like humans do. They have to have strong survival instincts, because they need it on the streets. But there were always fewer fights and less growling when Tina was around. She commanded respect without having a single aggressive bone in her body, and other dogs followed suit, becoming more gentle themselves.

She led by example, with her charm and charisma drawing everyone to her, without seemingly doing anything other than just being herself. I noticed this almost supernatural sense of peace, like a special aura, in the simplest moments such as during tea breaks with the team on the land.

Typically, I walk about 16 to 18 dogs when on my own. Tina would come on *every single* walk with me no matter which dog it was. She never once took a break. If I'd put one of those smart watches or a Garmin on her, I reckon she'd be clocking up doggie steps of around 30,000 a day.

I've long realised that educating the young about animal care should be an important priority. So when a local school asked me to come in and speak to the children, I was over the moon (if a little nervous if the truth be told, as schools and me were never a successful combo). The school principal asked me: 'Is there a gentle dog that would be friendly and safe with young children to meet?'

Of course I immediately knew who I'd take. So I did a little talk (which felt funny, standing in front of a bunch of kids being a 'responsible adult') with Tina dutifully at my feet. I'd planned a presentation of sorts, but within two minutes no child was listening – they were all stroking Tina while she stood there calm, patient and quite frankly lapping up the attention of 20 little hands petting her fluffy, soft fur and belly.

We drove home on the moped afterwards and I could tell she was tired from all that attention, as she rested her head on my leg and dozed off. It felt like we'd made a really important impact on those kids and they'd seen how kind souls dogs could be.

One of my very favourite things was getting to watch – and join in with – Tina swimming. We're lucky to have access to a beautiful beach here in Koh Samui, which being a European I never take for granted. And neither did Tina. She clearly adored the clear blue ocean and warm sand beneath her paws until the water lifted her making her weightless. Aaah … what true peace that feeling is.

Had she ever been in the water before we took her? I can never know for sure. With dogs, unlike babies and kids who take lessons, it's instinctive – her adorable doggy paddle just kicked in once her paws were no longer touching the sand. Watching her grin, pink tongue lolling in pleasure, her delight was obvious. It was as if all her problems just melted away …

I know myself that feeling. The sea is so vast it makes you appreciate the wonders of the world and how small so many of the things are in reality that cause us so much day-to-day stress.

Taking Tina out into the water became one of my most favourite things. It felt very special and even more indulgent in the evening times when sometimes just the two of us would paddle out into the sea following the horizon and

take a dip at the end of a long day. It became the very best way to wind down. Far more soothing than downing pints after work, and far cheaper (and more rewarding) than any therapy session.

There could have been a million things happening in the world – from nuclear bombs to global catastrophes – and the two of us splashing around with big silly grins on our faces couldn't have cared less in that moment.

CHAPTER EIGHT

WHEN BAD NEWS HITS US HARD

What then happened in the late spring really did threaten to test my mental health. We received the bad news we simply didn't want to hear. Just a few short months after we had found Tina, and had seemingly nursed her back to health with such care and devotion, we had more test results come back from the vet's, who diagnosed that Tina was suffering with stage 2 to 3 kidney failure.

The kidneys, as you probably know, are like the body's natural filters that do a lot of important things, like getting rid of waste from the bloodstream, keeping the right balance of essential minerals like potassium and sodium, saving water and, of course, making urine.

I'm neither a doctor nor a vet, so I won't get too medical with you here, but the term 'kidney failure' doesn't actually mean the kidneys have completely stopped working, it's more that the kidneys really aren't doing a great job filtering waste from the blood. And this is crucial to living healthily.

When a dog's kidneys start packing in, it certainly doesn't mean that they've stopped making urine altogether.

In fact, it's a bit ironic, because most dogs with kidney failure actually produce a lot of wee, but their bodies aren't getting rid of the toxic stuff like they should.

Unfortunately, kidney tissue in dogs (like in humans) doesn't ever grow back once it's damaged (unlike the liver which can regenerate a bit). And because the kidneys have a clever kind of 'back-up system', they could quietly be gradually getting worse for months, or even years, before anyone might realise there's a problem, and by that time only a fraction of the organ is properly functioning. Then you're in trouble.

In dogs, it's often just a part of getting older, the kidneys slowly wearing out over time, and when the symptoms show up is usually dependent on the size of the dog. It's very common. Bigger breeds of dog do tend to have shorter lifespans, but I felt certain that Tina's body had been put through so much stress when she was abused as a breeding dog and then left half-starving for dead, it would have created more health issues. Being so uncared for had sped up her worsened kidney function, I was sure of it.

Tina was constantly drinking water, which is generally the earliest sign of kidney trouble for dogs.

We were left reeling by the unwanted diagnosis. We asked multiple vets in Thailand for advice, and some overseas vets who'd heard about Tina's story online also offered their opinions and shared their expertise. But whoever we asked, the unanimous verdict was that Tina Turner – the brave little warrior she was – would have just three to six months to live.

It really was an awful blow. We'd all seen how much better she was doing since the rescue. We all so wanted her to get a happy ending and her very own forever home. She was certainly not short of admirers, or people who would have gladly offered her a family life.

She was so settled in with me, Snoop and Jumbo, I didn't know whether I could have actually borne to be parted from her.

The week of the diagnosis there were plenty of tears from all of us who had got to know and love Tina since her arrival. While I put on a stoic face delivering the bad news to all the volunteers, offering a shoulder to cry on, I was utterly gutted inside and went and had my own little cry back at the apartment.

Sometimes it just gets to you, doesn't it?

But I had to go into practical mode. I sought the expert advice of the vets for what we could now do in terms of end of life care. And we took every possible measure to get her living – and enjoying her life still – for as long as we possibly could.

We got Tina onto a special diet with fresh foods and fish and veg, we made sure she got all daily fluids injected so her kidneys didn't have to work as hard, we got her new medicines to make sure she was never in pain, and we made sure she had additional tests like ultrasounds and regular vet checks so we knew what was going on. I knew I wanted Tina to live as long as possible, but I never wanted her to be in pain.

I decided that although the news was terrible (and to be honest a shock – I'm such an optimist I wanted to defy the vets) I was determined to make whatever time Tina had left in this world as joyful as she deserved.

While all the humans who loved her were devastated, Tina was largely oblivious to the fact her time on this earth was limited. Or perhaps she knew but like a wise old person decided just to not care and to make the most of every day.

Seeing her and knowing we wouldn't have her for much longer made me very philosophical. I started all sorts of deep pondering on mortality and life – after all, *everyone's* time on this earth is limited. But most of us don't really confront the fact we will die at some point.

Once again, it reminded me of the fact that it was only when I was made to face my own mortality that I realised I wanted to live. I tried very hard in those days to reframe Tina's bad diagnosis as something that would bring positive change. I just didn't know what at that stage.

Despite the bad news we'd received, I knew I had to hold myself together at this time and I knew I needed to put some effort into meditating and exercising and staying well. Now was not the time to start spiralling into gloom – or give up hope.

Having the incredible support of so many people is what carries me some days. The outpouring of concern over this one little dog was staggering. One woman was so kind that she offered to pay for all Tina's veterinary care for the rest of her short life. I can't tell you what this enormous generosity meant to me.

With a condition as serious as Tina's kidney failure, we were all aware she wouldn't be here with us for as long as we wanted. But while we could maintain her energy levels she continued to be a bundle of love and pure joy, usually refusing to take a break from following her humans around. She played with her tennis balls, and gratefully enjoyed every minute she had left.

I promised to get Tina the comfiest bed and nicest food. 'She'll stay beside me for all her remaining time and we'll dream up some gentle adventures and moments for her,' I told everyone at the land. My role was to be strong, to make sure she had everything she needed, to spoil her. To see sunsets. To have beach trips. To make her feel like exactly what she was … the most special queen in the world.

Sometimes I would look back at the first video I'd ever made of Tina, on the day of her rescue, to remember how far she had come. If we hadn't found her that day, she would have died. Alone and without ever knowing love. All we could do now was try to do exactly what Tina did – live in the moment and not worry about tomorrow.

But however much I could philosophise and try to live in the present, it was truly heartbreaking seeing her health fail over that July. Her test results had been troubling for the past month, signalling that her health was now fast deteriorating despite us trying everything we could to prolong her life.

Every day, she carried on the dog walk rounds. Her spirit unbroken, and she always had a real fear of missing out the fun despite her illness. She didn't like being alone either, which to be honest suited me just fine as I wanted her around all the time anyway. She always wore a fresh, clean bandana, ate the best food and radiated happiness and contentment.

But then, one Thursday in August, something had definitely changed. For the first time Tina only came on one short walk, before retreating to rest in the office. This solitary behaviour was unprecedented for Tina.

I knew then that if Tina wasn't coming on a walk, she really was done – she no longer had the energy of her infectious zest for life. It was emotionally overwhelming to think about, but I knew we were inching closer to the time when we would have to say our goodbyes. I was quiet and distracted for the rest of the day, going through the motions but not fully present.

Then, when I returned after a long day sterilising other dogs and sorting out stuff on the land, with my takeaway dinner for that evening, Tina didn't get up to greet me as I came through the door. She would always rush up to greet me wagging her tail, delighted to see me (and me her) every time she heard the key in the door. When she didn't appear I froze for a few seconds. I suddenly didn't fancy the dinner I was still holding in my hand.

I knew this was significant even without any blood tests or a vet to confirm it. It was time to accept what was happening here. I put the takeaway down, my appetite was gone anyway, and I had a little moment to myself, steeling myself for the reality that Tina had given everything she had left to give. It wouldn't be long now. I held her closely that night, feeling her breathing, stroking her soft fur, holding her warm paddy paws in mine. And wondering what the next day would bring.

That day came and she didn't want to come to work with me. In fact she didn't want to move at all. I thought about encouraging her to come, even if it was only for a short walk to stretch her legs in the fresh air. But I thought better of it. It wouldn't have been right to put any more stress on her worn-out body. She stayed with me in the apartment and I didn't leave her side. I got help with other responsibilities so I could focus on Tina. I would duck out briefly to get food or help another dog, but did very little else – my priority was giving Tina every second I could.

And yes, it was for selfish reasons too: I just wanted to be there.

We used to lie on the couch together, and she would melt into my body in a way I can't fully explain. Dogs usually move around or adjust themselves, but she just moulded into whatever position I took. I would lie flat on my back, and she would lie on top of me, like a hug from above. She was absolutely exhausted, but she was so, so content. I could feel her happiness when she adopted that position. And I hoped that she in return could feel my love for her, too.

But it was Tina lying on my stomach in the hammock with me – outside the back of my place on the balcony – that will forever remain such a special memory. Her body was shutting down in those final hours but she didn't show any pain. Despite what must have been intense discomfort from kidney failure, she accepted her fate with grace. She was at peace with the world.

When it was time for her to go, I felt a weird sense of calm too. It was a clear blue sky, a summer's day, with only the occasional, brilliant white cloud gently making its way across the horizon. The sort of perfect day on an island you'd see in the pages of glossy travel magazines.

Two songs were playing on the radio below our hammock. One was 'Tiny Dancer', the 1971 classic by Elton John, with its gentle piano melody. I listened along, as did Tina, while she dozed in and out of consciousness.

The other was the beautiful 1995 hit 'Days Like This' by Van Morrison, a song I'd heard many times before, but now found myself listening to the soulful lyrics about the ups and downs of life, and the special days when everything seems to fall into place effortlessly, with more interest than I'd had before. The song emphasises the idea that even when life is challenging, there are moments when everything goes right.

It's a song full of optimism and resilience, two character traits that defined Tina so perfectly. It was the reminder I needed that life was still worth living, even though Tina was dying.

In those shared moments I had this very clear sense that life had to be enjoyed somehow, and that painful times were an important part of living. They couldn't be escaped, or blotted out with other things like alcohol (despite my previous best efforts). The acceptance of the hard times, I realised, makes us truly appreciate the joy in life too.

So if there was the best and most peaceful way for this much beloved retriever to pass away, it was sitting in a hammock, with wonderful music playing and being held tight by a human who truly loved her.

Tina slipped away quietly and gently at 4.45 that Friday afternoon, barely moving as Sybille, a good friend and a human doctor, was with me throughout. Tina's passing was as smooth as it can be. We said goodbye to beautiful Tina, and I'm so pleased that it was a peaceful – even happy – death. We made sure she was as comfortable as she could be.

It was by far the most profound moment in my life that I'd ever experienced. When eventually the rise and fall of Tina's soft belly grew still, Sybille and I looked at each other and knew. Without exchanging a word, Sybille understood that I needed to have some time alone now.

When it comes to burying the dead, different cultures have different traditions. Once we knew Tina's end was imminent I'd already arranged for a local handyman to dig a hole for her grave. You have to be practical, especially in a hot country like Thailand.

We debated whether to bury her right there and then or wait, but I decided it was better to do it immediately. I wanted – and needed – closure. This time had been coming for a while, and in that moment I felt that it was the right thing to do.

Tina's final resting place isn't in Giuseppe's Memorial Garden (a special burial place on the land, named after a very noble street dog called Giuseppe) with the other dogs who have passed. I wanted her to be buried under the hammock at the land, so her happy, positive spirit could infuse the place, and where I can sit and tell her about our ongoing mission to save street dogs around the world.

Lowering her golden body into the earth felt incredibly raw, and yes of course there were tears in my eyes. But there was also something about the manual labour involved in her burial that felt cathartic. Once again Sybille was sensitive enough to walk away and let me fill in the grave alone. I just didn't want anyone else to do it.

As I slowly covered the hole in the ground with every shovel of earth, then laid the final stones on the top, something deep inside me erupted. I let out a shout that was probably more like an animal kind of cry than a human noise. It wasn't directed at Tina, but at the world at large for treating animals as badly as it had. I shouted into the air at nobody in particular, 'Your life won't be in vain. I'll do something amazing in your name.'

I was angry and raw, the tears came thick and fast from my eyes, but I also had determined steel inside me. I spoke to Tina, telling her I would do so much work in her name. I was already on a mission to help street dogs, but this loss and then complete rage spurred me to a whole new level. I wouldn't be frightened of making bigger plans. It was something to drive me on: I needed to fulfil her legacy.

I placed flowers and then the tennis balls Tina had so loved on her grave, and I walked away knowing I had to use her death to achieve more for the dogs.

I knew everyone around the world who had followed Tina's story would be heartbroken by the news of her passing, but I was determined that her death should be viewed in a positive and joyful way. To remind us all she was a beacon of hope, kindness and love. And I'm so happy they felt the same for in the moments of announcing this loss, people started doing kind things for each other and posting stuff using #doingitfortina.

I asked people to just do something nice and kind for others. That was all. Whether it was just as simple as taking your dogs to the beach or a lake, or sending an old friend a kind message, or treating someone to a few Sunday drinks or pizza. Stop and talk to someone old and lonely, or even just hold a door open for someone. It made me smile, this idea of people who had never even met Tina all carrying out some small act of kindness and selflessness in her honour. Knowing she would have approved and might be smiling down from heaven with her wolfy grin and bandana.

But despite the brave face I was putting on, I have to admit, the next few weeks got to me. They were some of the hardest of my life. I missed her so much – her smell, her wet nose, her pretty face, lovely fur and changing her bandanas. Riding on the bike with her. *Everything.*

CHAPTER NINE

A DOUBLE BLOW

Only a week or so after losing Tina, in what felt like a very cruel double blow, I had to say another sad goodbye to a very old and dear friend. Snoop was my very first dog, the beloved labrador cross who I'd rescued years earlier in Ireland. He'd been with me when I first moved to Thailand, and the one friend I'd relied on when I was drinking and depressed, full of despair and self-loathing and not wanting to carry on. Just having his warm, non-judgemental presence there during those miserable times was the only thing that kept me going some days.

He was old and his body had been giving in for a while, so I'd sensed it would be time to say goodbye for a few months before it actually happened. But as much as I'd been preparing myself, it's still gut wrenching when it happens. This time I was losing the most incredibly precious and loyal old friend ever. He was the sort of dog who didn't need to jump around or lick you non-stop for your attention. You could open a book or sit and look at the sunset and he'd lay beside you exuding love, confident in his place and at ease with all around him.

While there wasn't anything drastically wrong with Snoop, like a specific organ failure or cancer or anything like that, two of his vertebrae were slowly fusing together, so he was struggling to walk and becoming more frail and immobile over about the period of a year.

He'd gone from reasonably long walks to 500 metres then to 100, and then down to 50. It wasn't just how far he couldn't walk, he was beginning to have falls and hurt himself on the furniture. I'd worked hard to make my apartment safe for him, moving chairs around and putting softer rugs down to cushion any falls. I guess that's what parents do when they have crawling babies and toddlers: you need eyes in the back of your head to spot potential dangers and anticipate them before accidents happen.

Snoop's spirits were still very good. He could sit around all day without getting anxious or fretful, and he enjoyed being beside me at my desk. We would still go on short walks and I would drive him up to the land. He was very happy sitting there too, always in his own place, still eagerly taking the world in and seemingly interested in new dogs coming and going.

During the time I was incredibly stressed. In the end, I committed to writing my book so every free moment I had was spent trying to put words down. It was mostly about my life and once I'd opened the box I thought I'd closed decades ago, it felt like I was in freefall into an unknown torrent of emotions. I would be staying up late to finish the chapters. All the while Snoop was by my side with his health deteriorating. I was helpless. He was my life. He is the only being that knew me from the start. He was someone I could not hide from and someone who never judged me throughout all I put us through. I needed him to pull through, and help me one more time. A tumour had come up on his neck, it had become engorged with blood almost overnight and then exploded one evening. At the time of night that it popped, the vets were all closed so I spent a long and anxious night squeezing out the blood gently and dabbing it off with gauze. Sometimes the blood would come out faster and I'd have to put pressure on it rather than squeeze it. We just about kept him alive overnight, squeezing, dabbing, pressurising, and got him to a vet first thing in the morning. They were able to quickly cut out and clean up whatever it was, and after he'd been neatly stitched up he was pretty stable.

At least for another few months he seemed well enough, if somewhat more diminished. His little falls were becoming more frequent and he began to become incontinent, too, bless him. He would have accidents in the night, pooping himself and wetting the floor. And because it would mostly happen overnight when I was sleeping, Snoop would spend the night sliding around in the poo and smearing it around the floor as well as up the walls. So waking up to this in the mornings was grim, as you can imagine.

This period of caring for Snoop gave me such an insight into the hard and complicated emotions of being a carer, along with a massive respect for everyone who cares for loved ones, and the people who choose careers in the caring profession. You'd need a big heart and a lot of patience.

I couldn't help but get annoyed with poor Snoop after he'd had an accident. I know it wasn't his fault, he was old, but I would wake up, see the mess and think, *Really? Again?!* Having that flash of irritation with my great friend, when he was at his weakest, made me feel like such a bad person. It still haunts me now, that fleeting frustration about something that Snoop could not control. I wish I'd been better in those moments. I know that guilt will never leave me.

How could I get angry and irritated at him? I knew I'd let him down and wasn't doing enough for him. But I'd also be conscious of the fact I needed to get on with the day and plough through the huge to-do list in my head, and then I would feel mean and selfish for putting my needs first while also a bit frustrated and resentful about the impact all the caring was having on my wellbeing. Everything was becoming rather negative in my mind and I became trapped in this cycle.

I'd just lost Tina and in my heart I knew Snoop wouldn't be here for much longer. On top of that, I was due to go to England for the publication of my first book, which I called

called *Hope*. I'd committed to doing a round of publicity and, typical me, I'd told the team there to cram in as much as possible.

It felt a big deal, and after saying yes to flying over I felt I couldn't let people down. ITV asked if I would go on their show called *This Morning* and a bunch of other interviews and activities were booked up and down the country. In fact there was a whole schedule lined up which was going to be great for the project and the dogs. But I was already feeling fragile about Tina's death and now Snoop was taking a turn for the worse, I wondered if I had bitten off more than I could chew?

Everyone who knows me knows that I don't go in for half measures – I throw myself into things wholeheartedly. Yet even though I had seen Snoop with this bloody tumour on his neck, and I had seen him become less sure on his paws and now incontinent, I still didn't think it was time to let him go yet.

Not everyone agreed with me. You might have heard people say, or you might have lived it yourself, that you know when the moment is right to put a pet down. And while it's very, very hard to know when you've reached that moment, I truly felt that I wasn't quite there yet with Snoop.

I receive and read a lot of comments on social media. I have learned over the years to treat most of the negative stuff as water off a duck's back, but I have always got a bit upset and annoyed when people message me saying it's time to put a dog down. There were quite a few people saying this kind of thing with Snoop at that time, and in the emotional state I was in, that made me more angry and upset than ever, because I was thinking, *I've been with this dog for 12 years. We've been through thick and thin. I will know when the time is right, thank you.* I didn't say that publicly, it's never wise to get into a debate or react with your heart on social media, but it was boiling under during that period – and I was due to leave for the UK in just four days' time.

It was such a tough few days. One minute I'd look at him and think, *He's got another two months in him, it'll be fine*, and then immediately I'd think, *I can't leave him at the end of his life, after everything we've been through – what happens if he passes and I'm not there to hold his paw and stroke his head?*

It got to the stage where I had decided that Snoop was more important, and in my mind I resolved that I would cancel the trip to the UK for the book launch. *It's just a book and a stupid trip to England. I could easily do the interviews from Thailand on the phone or online.* In the grand scheme of things, I stood a chance of missing out on the passing of somebody who'd been beside me through such major events.

So with that decision now firmly set in my mind, Snoop and I fell into a routine. I would wake up, clean up any toilet mishaps he'd had overnight and then lift him out onto the edge of my balcony, where there was a bit of a morning suntrap. The old boy would sit there for a couple hours, soaking up the rays and I would be up and down doing little things, including going down to get a coffee and my breakfast. And that was where I was in the routine one morning. I had been gone from the apartment for about 15 minutes to get my coffee and pastries (caffeine and sugar fix were needed in my mornings). When I look back now, I feel as if when I walked back up the hill I could almost feel something different in my bones as I returned home.

When I walked back into the flat, I knew. I knew immediately that now was the time that I had to say goodbye to Snoop. Out of nowhere, he had started panting and it was clear he couldn't get up – his legs were paddling against the floor but he was unable to lift his weight up. I helped him up and could see how out of breath he was. I looked him dead in the eye – God I loved this animal – and he blinked his dark eyes gently as he gazed back. It felt like he was giving a sign or some kind of permission. A lump rose at the back of my throat as I realised that now the time had come.

Over the course of the day, his deterioration, which had been slow and inexorable over days, quickened to him worsening by the hour. By that evening, I decided it was time to summon the vet.

However, that bloody dialogue started up in my head again, ricocheting between me knowing the end had now come for Snoop and then thinking that I was jumping the gun and just wanting to have him put to sleep because I had to go to England.

It was a real internal conflict spiking in my head and going round in circles, but when I focused and thought back to the morning – the state he had been in when I had come back from buying breakfast and found him – I knew that this was not a dog who was enjoying himself anymore. I knew Snoop better than I think I've ever known anyone or anything, and I could see he was miserable, in pain and struggling. If I wasn't around, he wouldn't have been able to look after himself.

When I could focus on things in these terms, I knew it was time. I felt strongly that I didn't want anyone else with me for the moment of his passing.

What surprised me then, and still surprises me now, is that when he passed it was actually a good moment. I didn't cry, I held his paw, looked into his eyes and he slipped away. I was very happy for him to have had such a wonderful life and such calm and peaceful surroundings for most of his time on this earth.

Snoop's death was very much a time for quiet reflection about the wonderful life he'd had, and ultimately the wonderful life he'd given me as I wouldn't be here today if it wasn't for him. That was something private between us, and I looked into his eyes as he was passing and thanked him personally for that in a very deep way.

I mentioned specific times when I had been drinking and depressed, when just seeing him do something or wander into the room I was in had massively helped me. So many things started playing in my mind: when I sold my company, when I moved to Manchester, and then Thailand, when I'd been slumped at my dinner table surrounded by empty bottles of wine, my big break-up.

I spoke about some of those times to him, when I was trying to stay sober through exercise and he'd been there jogging alongside me on 10 km runs, and about how looking down at his little wheeling legs always gave me fresh energy, but most of all I thanked him, and hoped he'd enjoyed his life as much I had enjoyed him being a part of mine.

I strongly believe he understood.

I buried him myself in the middle of the night when all around me was still, but for the gentle breeze in the air ringing from the trees. As I lowered him into the ground to take his place next to Tina, I stood over him and quietly let my mind drift in that moment.

I had shared a lot about Tina online, but with Snoop I kept a little bit back and didn't share quite as much. Obviously, I put up a heartfelt post about his passing but only did so after I had sat with my sadness for two or three days. I wanted to keep it all a little more private as it was something for me to process and deal with personally.

TINA

Nobody really knew me as well as Snoop. On the flipside nobody knew Snoop as well as I did. I wanted to keep it that way.

Tina and the others were very much everybody's dogs online, and everybody could have a piece of their lives, but for Snoop and I, it was personal, we'd been through it all together and I didn't need to share that grief, *my* grief, with the whole world like I did with Tina. This grief felt like my thing to deal with and that would have paradoxically been made harder if lots of people had been wishing me well and sending me their sympathy. I know that sounds so weird but maybe you know what I am talking about if you've lived through grief.

Quite naturally people are curious about what we do with the dogs after they have died. Currently, we do all the aftercare for them ourselves. Clearly, we aren't able to cremate the animals so we bury them. The major practical consideration here is digging the hole for a dog's final resting place. We have to dig them deep because otherwise other dogs can pick up the scent and will be drawn to the area where we lay a lot of the dogs to rest. We haven't had a scenario where they have started digging or anything like that, but it is a bit sad and morbid if the other dogs are hanging around that area looking distracted.

Obviously Thailand is a hot and humid country. We don't have refrigeration facilities so we look to act quickly and I think that's right with regards to the dogs' dignity too.

I think in cultures where there is a bit of a delay before burying the departed it's to allow extended family to be able to pay their respects and say farewell. So here in Thailand we are a tight-knit community and maybe that's less important. Speaking as someone who is in recovery from alcoholism and has had their ups and downs with their mental health, I find that culture difficult. You can go and have a few drinks and be surrounded by friends, family, and interesting acquaintances and reminisce about someone that you all remember fondly.

But it's the aftermath I have a problem with. Everybody goes home where you're on your own with your grief and your memories and maybe with the added vulnerability of being hungover, and that is hard and rarely spoken about.

Now I look back on it, I think I was holding myself together because of the impending trip and I knew I couldn't afford to let the wave of emotion overwhelm me before then. I consciously bottled it up. I knew that if I let it out at all I might just have to curl up into a ball and cry for six months. So I kept it all inside me and headed off to England.

CHAPTER TEN

ALL IN FOR TINA

Considering the emotional toll both Tina's and Snoop's deaths had taken on me, my trip to the UK couldn't have come at a better time in some ways. It was better for me to escape to England, where I could be kept on a frantically busy schedule, rather than mope about at home, drowning in memories. The sight of the empty sofa, where I had grown accustomed to seeing one or the other curled up and sleeping, struck me like a physical blow every time I walked past it. Each pang of loss was a stark reminder of my grief. I didn't want to be in my own house anymore. I decided to get out.

So, that's what I did. Catching a flight turned out to be a refreshing novelty, an invigorating experience that lifted my spirits. In recent years, I hadn't bothered taking many holidays; if I needed a break to recharge, I'd simply treat myself to a weekend in a hotel in Thailand. However, the enforced solitude on the plane provided an unexpected gift – a moment to reflect on Tina's death and my heartfelt promise to her in her final hours to make her life matter. In my anguish, I had sworn aloud to her that her life wouldn't be in vain.

I realised I wouldn't let her down on this promise. For several months, I had been contemplating ways to help animals in need, and Tina's passing became the catalyst I needed.

I thought long and hard about what would be the best way to honour her. I thought about the many dogs we had helped, rescued and sadly lost. I was raw with anger at how Tina had been treated but that was in the past – the present was how we dealt with it. And then I realised how many people were involved in her recovery, how many trips to the vets we had taken and how in that lonely hour when her stomach had swollen to fatal levels and we were lost and confused, we had nowhere to go. We needed a place of our own where we can treat sick dogs. We needed to have it available round the clock. And we needed it today. A Tina hospital is exactly what we needed.

Our mission got a new name too – Happy Doggo – and in order to be as effective as possible we were also in the laborious process of registering it as a charity.

Getting charity status was so important to me. We're so passionate about what we do, but now things were going to be noted on record. Being recognised as a charity is a huge boost, for not only does it give our work credibility but it also means that all the kind people and organisations that want to support us can feel that it's above board and genuine. It's more than just our reputation, it's the trust people put in us, and I felt it was absolutely essential we have this. I always want to make it clear that everything is for the dogs, and not for any bad humans who might keep the profit for themselves. And certainly not for me. People are so kind and giving and now they can feel totally assured they're contributing to a recognised cause.

Charities often get a lot of positive attention which can help spread the word about your mission. Again, as far as Happy Doggo is concerned we use social media a lot which helps with visibility and sharing our efforts, but overall registering as a charity is a good thing and worth the effort for what we need to achieve.

Happy Doggo Land is the ideal place for dogs needing refuge from the streets, somewhere clean and safe so that with human support they can find cosy shelter until they regain their health.

Initially, the land was just an empty space in part of the jungle, accessed via a dirt track, the little lane leading from the main road. Until a kind-hearted supporter crafted and sent a special handmade road sign with the name 'Hope Avenue: where dogs' dreams come true' emblazoned across it. It felt like the perfect name for this previously nondescript path, so-called in honour of the rescue dog Hope who also inspired the book. It also symbolised exactly what we aimed to achieve: a beacon of hope for those who needed it the most. Everyone could use a little more hope in their lives, especially dogs who arrived battered and weary, where hope was essential for recovery and outlook on the future.

The land was flourishing. I ran my small office from an old shipping container – nothing flashy, but it got the job done. The dogs had a little sanctuary, and I managed the business side of operations, coordinated volunteers, oversaw the (rapidly expanding) sterilisation programme, and ensured fresh food was prepared.

By now, we were feeding one thousand dogs daily with wholesome meals packed with nutritious ingredients like veggies, chicken, rice, coconut oil and eggs. I had enlisted one incredibly hardworking local woman to manage the central kitchen, which meant that other dog lovers who wanted to help could collect meals and distribute them to street animals without having to cook at home. This streamlined approach significantly improved the dogs' overall health, reducing our long-term need for medical expenses, as healthier dogs were more resilient to infections.

Seeing the dogs relish their freshly roasted chicken and pumpkin risotto, served on palm leaves, brought joy to my heart. Yet, as I settled into this routine, I began contemplating the next steps. It seemed clear that my initial idea of establishing a clinic on the island would be the logical progression. A facility where we could sterilise dogs, administer vaccinations and provide active medical treatment was a dream worth pursuing. I had jotted down rough calculations in my mind, and later sketched them on paper, but the total seemed staggering. Just setting up a basic clinic would likely cost around $150,000, and then I would need to consider staffing it …

I made sure to visit Tina and Snoop before I left, and laid flowers on both their graves. I mulled over this ambitious idea, speaking softly to Tina, convinced she was listening from doggy heaven. The notion of establishing a hospital for dogs who were struggling felt daunting, almost impossibly ambitious. Yet, I understood that having a dedicated space to care for these vulnerable animals could make a life-saving difference. This goal was worth pursuing, and I vowed that somehow I would prioritise making it happen upon my return. I promised Tina I would do that. A hospital on the land where all good dogs could get help. I had no intention of letting her down.

Being back in England certainly felt a little surreal. The air smelled like my old feeling of being at home – both familiar and yet so different. And unusually for the UK, it wasn't actually cold – and neither was it raining! It was a warm September day, and once I landed on the tarmac and ditched my bag at the hotel that would serve as my base here, I felt all itchy feet. I'm useless with nothing to do as I'm kept busy every hour of the day in Thailand.

I hadn't made any plans because I'd seen the media schedule and knew we had a lot to cover in the next few days. So it was a spur-of-the-moment decision to send a message to my followers, 'Let's do a walk in Hyde Park.' Hyde Park is a beautiful green space in the centre of London, home to Speakers' Corner, the Serpentine lake where people swim and Princess Diana's memorial playground. It was conveniently close to my hotel. Given the lovely weather, I just wanted to bring a few people together. In times past, I would have been tempted by a beer garden of a pub, but I didn't want that anymore; I still felt a longing for community. I posted that if anyone wanted to come down after work and bring their dog, I'd be there.

Honestly, I didn't expect many to turn out, but if a handful showed up with their four-legged friends, I thought it would be a worthwhile experience and a nice way to connect. The culture surrounding a wake after a funeral – sharing happy memories and celebrating a life – was on my mind. I felt an urge to create this kind of gathering in the UK to joyfully honour Tina. She had touched so many lives here too.

What really surprised me was that people actually turned out – in droves! On that day in London, despite the short notice, around 300 people came, many bringing their pets. I think this turnout was a testament to how people perceived it as a celebration of Tina's life. While I had kept Snoop's passing low-key, those who knew me understood how profound that loss had been.

I was absolutely blown away, to tell you the truth. The fact that so many strangers joined, each with their dogs, truly put a massive smile on my face. For me, a walk was always my go-to when grappling with depression or anxiety. Sometimes, as I've said, the weight of depression can be so heavy that even the thought of going for a walk seems impossible. But somehow, if you can manage to pull open the curtains and step outside, everything changes.

Many people approached me, sharing their own stories about their dogs and how following the ups and downs of street dogs in Thailand had brought them joy from afar. They expressed their condolences for Tina's passing, and I was moved to learn how much hope they had harboured for her recovery. I couldn't believe how many cared.

Some people opened up about their own dark days, illnesses and personal battles. A few had photos of their favourite dogs – like McMuffin, the courageous little beagle cancer survivor we all adored – saved on their phones. They shared how witnessing dogs' resilience inspired them to keep pushing through tough times. Many simply wanted to connect, to be part of something larger, and watching strangers strike up conversations filled my heart with joy.

All of it truly amazed me. Some even messaged me afterwards, saying they hadn't felt brave enough to approach me but were grateful they attended. The London walk had been such a success that when I travelled to

Manchester for the publicity tour, I tweeted a similar message. Even more people showed up, around 500 to 600 this time. Again, the fine weather likely played a role, and I couldn't help but think that Tina and Snoop had something to do with the delightful sunshine.

In Manchester, I chose the Chorlton Ees Nature Reserve, a lovely green space where Snoop and I used to walk when I lived in the city. I remembered those challenging days when I fought through my lows, Snoop loyally jogging by my side, regardless of the weather, which you had to be prepared for, as it frequently rained there.

I still think about some of the people I met. One person had worked a night shift at Asda, finished at 3 a.m., then swiftly got into their car and travelled all the way from Cornwall, right in the southwest corner of England, just to join us in Liverpool. I was speechless. I didn't know if I deserved such a reception but I knew that the dogs had moved something big in people's hearts and minds, and the dog that they all felt for the most was of course Tina. So when another special attendee came up to me in Manchester holding a handmade felt model of Tina, I was so overwhelmed with emotion I didn't know what to do. As I held this delicate and unique creation in my hand, taking in all the detail it had – the bandana, the tail, the eyes – I saw it truly captured Tina's spirit in full. It must have taken this lady hours to create, and it was astonishingly lifelike, complete with a tiny tennis ball. I was so moved I could barely utter my appreciation to her. I've always been overwhelmed by the thoughtful gifts people bring and send. In fact, I ended up filling five suitcases with presents that had to be shipped to me later because I couldn't carry them all back on the flight. There were t-shirts with Tina's face, handwritten cards, chocolate bars, Tina flip-flops, bandanas for Derek, treats for Jumbo – it was incredible.

What I cherish about these gifts is that they weren't extravagant; most were created with genuine love and heart. The drawings from children, in particular, always bring a lump to my throat. These same kids often tell me they're donating their pocket money that week to help feed a street dog. Oh my goodness, my heart swells when they say that.

Then, in Dublin, I went to Phoenix Park, where I also used to run regularly with Snoop. This time, the gathering of dog lovers swelled to about 2,000 people, I kid you not. It was so casual, people just gathered at the start of their evening, but it felt like a warm and special celebration that meant the world to me. People of all ages mingled, talking, petting dogs and making new friends. I think the weather truly makes a difference. In Thailand, we take sunshine for granted, but when it shines in England and Ireland, everyone seems to be in an exceptionally good mood, happy to be outside. It creates a carnival atmosphere, fostering a friendlier vibe.

However, the unexpectedly large turnout did get me into a bit of trouble with the local police. They noticed the crowd and approached, asking if I had applied for a permit for the gathering. Of course, I hadn't – oops. I had to play a bit dumb and apologised, insisting, 'I honestly didn't know it would get so big.' I promised to be more aware next time, and fortunately the potentially tricky citation was diffused. How could the officers not be won over by all those happy people and joyful dogs? Soon, they were patting the dogs and getting involved too. Sorry, officers, but some things are worth bending the rules for.

CHAPTER ELEVEN

IN THE EYE OF A
MEDIA STORM

The book tour was a whirlwind of busyness – interviews, book signings, talking and meeting people all day. Not my comfort zone, but I enjoyed not having time to think about things as well as the change of scenery. It still felt mad, if I'm honest, that I'd managed to write a book at all. Me, Niall Harbison, the boy with barely any qualifications.

I'd always been an avid reader at school, but I was so often getting into trouble that I ended up leaving with barely any exam certificates to my name. That's why I became a chef really. I think my poor dad was worried I wouldn't be able to do anything at all, so encouraged me to learn a trade. Every parent wants their kids to be able to make a living and live independently. And I admit it felt weird when all my school friends went off to universities. I couldn't help feeling like I was the 'thick' one being left behind. I didn't think it was true necessarily, but you carry those insecurities around in your head.

I think the teachers back in the day wrote me off as hopeless, or stupid, because I hadn't been able to knuckle down like most other kids. But I'd always loved reading about the world and doing my own kind of learning. I was naturally curious about histories, war, different cultures and famous people in power who had influence over how we live. And I still love reading today. Often when I walk the dogs I have a podcast or audio book on the go as I tend to fall asleep from exhaustion when my head hits the pillow.

Yet finding the time to write the book had not been easy. I spent some late nights beavering away at it, rethinking my whole life and how I'd got here. From a schoolboy in Belgium, to a chef in Dublin, to a media businessman in England … and now here I was, a bald Irish man in flip-flops on a mission to save street dogs. Well, it's not the most obvious career path, is it?

It was a cathartic experience in many ways, dredging up uncomfortable parts of my life and painful memories. And it instilled some discipline in my busy mind, sitting down at my laptop and trying to order my thoughts. Really going back over all parts of my life and the things that had been perhaps too painful to dwell on before.

I found it extremely difficult to confront those things from my youth and generally the first half of my entire life. It was painful to finally understand how that had negatively affected so many areas for me – from work to my (disastrous) relationships with women. I ended up hurting a lot of people. I have made heartfelt apologies since and I'm very lucky to now have great friendships with most of my exes (who are so kind and brilliant, and I'm happy to say have gone on to have very sorted lives without me constantly causing chaos). I'm also on great terms with my parents and my younger step-siblings. (My dad went on to have another two sons and my mum had a daughter – they are all wonderful.)

Mostly I was proud that I'd actually done the book, completed writing it on time and got it published. That in itself is an achievement but what it also taught me was that writing was so integral to processing your feelings. If you're ever stuck, write down how you're feeling, start your story in earnest. Try to capture in as many words as it takes how you feel in that moment. If you remember something from your past, good or bad, write it down. I promise the act of writing words down, any words, will bring you comfort. Do not get hung up on whether anyone would find it interesting or worry that it doesn't make sense or reads well. This is as much for you as for anyone else. Give it a go – you won't regret it. I guess that's why I'm sat here writing my second book.

However, here's the unexpected bit. Whereas writing the book had felt like an achievement, having to record the audio book was pure torture. And I mean *torture*. Imagine being locked in a soundproofed booth with headphones and a screen with your whole warts and all life displayed in neat lines. I truly hadn't appreciated how hard it would be to read out all the things I'd written in private. In the long hours with Snoop curled up at my feet, recording the audio made me cringe and even want to cry at times. For a week I stayed in Bangkok and for five or six hours a day I was in that sound booth reading out some of the darkest experiences of my life, line by uncomfortable line.

Every so often the audio guy was like 'just say that again, please,' and the line in question would be something about me drinking: 'Then, I got a Coke bottle and emptied it and topped the rest of it with Thai whiskey.' Things like that. And on top of everything else, they'd play back 30 seconds each time so I'd get my voice in my ear on a loop, over and over. I'd work myself into a state, convinced I would be slated and it would get a one-star review. But now I can just about laugh how funny that moment in the hot booth was.

In the end, it felt right to say yes to the audio because if I'd asked for an actor to read it instead, well, that wouldn't have made much sense as I appear and talk in the videos I share online. I just had to put up with listening to my own awful voice sounding like an idiot.

Talking about the drinking and my relationships obviously wasn't fun, but I remember reading one chapter out about a dog called Tyson, one of the first ones who died in my care, who had a real impact on me, and I found myself desperately trying not to cry in the studio in front of the sound engineers.

I'd get out after doing that and feel utterly drained and want to get straight into bed afterwards. That probably makes me sound like a real prima donna I know, I'm sorry.

It wasn't a comfortable experience but I felt it was necessary and important to do. I'd put in the effort of writing and recording it and the least I could do was try and promote the thing that might raise cash for the hospital. The more people who read about the dogs in the book, or downloaded it to listen to, the better, I reasoned. And with the ambition of the hospital in Tina's name now firmly in mind, I'd raised the bar of what would be needed. Here's how I saw it. This was going to not only help dogs but help them in a big way. This was the only viable route to building it.

The publishers were always very supportive and no-one pressured me to have such a heavy promotion schedule; it was me insisting I wanted to jam pack more in. They said, 'You're crazy, like, nobody does this amount of stuff,' but I figured that I wasn't in this part of the world often, and yet I had so much support here. If there was any way of showing my appreciation for the massively generous people, who helped the dogs so much, and made me personally feel so loved and supported, then I wanted to work my arse off for them.

It was of course strange being away from Thailand and all the dogs back home. And yes of course I worried and thought about them. But it's not quite like being a parent of teenagers while across the other side of the world, and how that must feel. For a start it's not like the dogs were going to have a massive rave-up with me out the country

… though McMuffin likes to be the life and soul of any gathering!

No, in all seriousness, I have excellent people who help on the land and with everything I do with the dogs. I can't stress enough that I have so much support from so many big hearted people and passionate animal lovers. I always get far too much credit for what I do and it's embarrassing sometimes. There is an army of us on the island all mucking in – we're a team. I'm not so important myself that if I go away for a week or so things fall apart in my absence. Nope, I go away and it's all super-organised and things kind of run themselves.

So it was all perfectly fine for me to focus on the task in hand. For seven days in a row it was non-stop. London, Manchester, Liverpool, Milton Keynes, Dublin, Blackburn, the Wirral: it became a blur of driving, flying and hotel rooms. I spoke to so many different journalists at different newspapers, and radio stations and TV too.

One of the highlights though was appearing on *This Morning*. Sitting on the couch, I felt I was on a completely different planet. The whole situation felt so odd and strange to me. The heat of the studio floor lights and knowing that the cameras were on me, recording everything live, made me feel so exposed. If it came across like it was somebody else answering the questions, well, maybe it was because they were – I do not remember any of it as I seemed to have this out-of-body experience and was looking down on this weird scene from above. At least that's how it felt. I was on autopilot, talking, talking, talking, when I heard someone say: 'We have a very special guest here for you.'

And out walked little Hope and her wonderful mum Steff who had adopted her. They crossed the floor so gently, you could tell Hope was feeling the same way I was, timidly but bravely approaching me. I thought I was prepared for the moment but, boy, was I wrong. Completely by surprise and out of nowhere the tears just started flooding out. Suddenly there wasn't a large morning audience watching, there were no presenters or TV crew in the studio. There was only myself and Steff and Hope. How in the world was it possible that she had been shot with a nail gun not that long ago but made it to a TV studio in London? And her little tail wagging as she recognised me, that just finished me off.

As the presenters finished up and we were ushered out, I needed to sit down somewhere quiet, but just as I was getting ready to head back to the room two crew members with headphones whispered to me, 'You better come and see this, there are some people waiting outside for you.'

Still wiping the tears from my eyes and trying to get myself together, I remember being absolutely blinded by the bright sunshine as the large backstage doors opened. I was thinking a couple of people must have seen the segment on TV and come from their houses around the corner to say hello. So I was completely and utterly baffled by the sight in front of me.

There was indeed a large group of people with their dogs. I looked at their smiling faces and thought, 'Wow, isn't this amazing … good, kind dog people are here.' It was only when I looked down at the dogs themselves that I nearly had a heart attack and let out a gasp of sheer astonishment. It was Whacker, one of the dogs I'd saved in Thailand. And there was Moritz! And Lottie. And little Rodney, but not so little anymore. Turns out they'd all organised this secretly between them. I had to laugh imagining King Whacker of Scotland getting on the woof phone to call up Rodders in Wales to see if he'd be up for a road trip to London. 'It's fine, mate, we can bunk at Moritz's in London, no sweat.' I think it is easily one of the most amazing and surreal moments in my life.

I don't remember much more than a big rush of both human and canine limbs as a scrum of happiness ensued. Again I went into a sort of autopilot mode as I zoned out in amazement, just looking around and trying to hold it together. This wasn't a case of me being anti-social or an introvert this time, but rather me being maybe the happiest and most fulfilled I've ever been in my life and being in genuine shock at something like this happening to me. Your dreams aren't really meant to come true in life, but in that moment seeing all those happy faces, they really were.

And of course this trip meant there was a chance to enjoy some of the things that I don't have so much in Thailand. Like staying in hotels meant I got breakfast included every morning, and hotel breakfasts are one of my favourite things. I can't resist a full English (or full Irish) or eggs Benedict or any of those lovely things you might have as a treat at weekends. So that was a nice little luxury.

It had all been such a whirlwind that I hadn't sat still with my thoughts for one moment during the tour. But on the last big event I was caught out. It was in Blackburn of all places, and a big old school with a large auditorium had been booked for a person, like a BBC journalist type of figure, to talk to me on stage about my life and work with a Q&A at the end.

It was all fine, and I was relieved I'd got through to the end of the tour in one piece and not broken down about Tina or Snoop. But then in the last 10 minutes, when the floor was opened up for people to ask me questions, somebody stood up and said, 'I don't have a question for Niall, but I wanted to just thank you for everything, and how Tina and Snoop have touched us all.'

Well, that was it. In front of about 500-odd people I just broke down in tears and started crying. I managed to choke out some sort of incomprehensible answer and try and recover my composure a little. Then out of the corner of my eye I saw a group of teenagers in the audience, dabbing their eyes with tissue. That set me off again! I felt a real big old weepy idiot in front of all those people, but I'd just been holding it in and holding it in, and my emotions caught up with me I guess and there was no holding them back that time.

Two days later, once I'd said my goodbyes and given big hugs to friends and family, I was on the plane to Thailand and very much ready to be reunited with everyone at Happy Doggo Land and firmly back in my comfort zone. I had important work to do. The hospital must happen. I was quickly realising that the hospital had to happen. Not just for Tina but for all the beautiful people who were now part of our journey and our story. This was also for them!

CHAPTER TWELVE

A SUPERMODEL COMES TO THE LAND (SORT OF)

*'When someone leaves it's because someone
else is about to arrive.'*

I think it was the Brazilian novelist Paulo Coelho who wrote that line, and I reckon it's a wise observation about loss – and how life carries on. In a similar way as when you grieve a person, it's not like you instantly get over losing a dog who has meant something to you, but life moves forward regardless. It's less about 'moving on' but being forced to 'move forward'. That's how it has to work. And there's always more dogs in dire need that require TLC and some sorting out.

One of the dogs who arrived at the land was Cindy Crawford, and what a little character she turned out to be.

Most dogs I come across every day in Thailand are severely malnourished and absolutely starving. They've only survived this long by fighting off other dogs for every scrap of food that they're lucky enough to be thrown or what they've managed to scavenge for. Beggars quite literally can't be choosers.

So Cindy Crawford (as she later became known) was a little different in that respect. I'd actually driven past her, a sort of brown and white shaggy dog, a few months earlier and noticed with some sadness she was overweight. But when there are so many suffering animals – many with far unhappier lives – you have to make quick judgement calls about which of them need to be the priority when it comes to stepping in with care or scooping them up and driving them on my moped to the vets. Otherwise I literally would not achieve anything in the grand plan to save thousands. This dog wasn't gaunt or thin in the slightest. Quite the opposite.

But it was only in the same month when I'd returned from the UK trip and I was driving around with some rare time to kill before a meeting, when I clocked her again and realised it was now time to swoop in and do something. And let me tell you, there was no way this four-legged lady was getting on any moped. She was properly obese.

There's no rhyme or reason when it comes to naming dogs. It's not like a number plate on a car or done alphabetically like hurricanes are named with the weather. They're picked at random, on a whim, because of how they look or behave, who they remind us of, or just something about their spirit that shines through. Or simply makes us chuckle.

When I was growing up in the 1990s, an Irish kid living in Brussels, Cindy Crawford was the stunning supermodel who seemed to grace every magazine cover including my bedroom walls. I didn't think that a prettier woman existed.

Well, this poor dog in front of me was the very opposite of all that, so it made people smile a bit when they asked her name. I was never poking fun, everything is meant with love and affection, but it keeps us a bit amused I suppose when times are tough. (I've also had dogs called Kate Moss, Ryan Gosling, Beyoncé and Nicole Kidman to name a few.)

Everything about Cindy Crawford the dog seemed down in the dumps and a little depressing. This was a street dog that was in a real pickle. Using her natural instinct to survive, Cindy had chosen to live in between a 7-Eleven store, the local corner shops that are ubiquitous in Koh Samui, and some restaurants. It wasn't that far from where I'm based myself. Clearly shops and food joints produce a lot of leftovers, and Cindy was smart enough to have cottoned on to these fringe benefits.

She was well known to the locals and everybody in the area was feeding her because she was such a friendly soul. Some dogs however – exactly like some of us humans – don't have an 'off switch' when it comes to their appetite. She had probably taken people offering her food as a sign she was loved, and who can blame her for hoovering up any kind of affection along with the food she was being offered?

But by the time I found her that September morning I could clearly tell she was in trouble. She was lying in the middle of the road, with her head close to the passing cars and exhaust fumes, and – I'm sorry to be rude – but she was looking less like a dog and more like a giant lead balloon. It wasn't just the weight that shocked me, but the fact that she was missing a load of her fur, too.

She was so overweight that when I tried to move her even just a yard off the road away from the cars to safety, well, initially I couldn't. I'm not 20 anymore alas. I haven't got a body-builder type of physique and I didn't want to do my back in.

Thankfully, a kind Thai woman came along to my aid, and the two of us together sort of managed to lift her off the road – me heaving and groaning and nearly doing myself an injury several times – where I could take a better look at her. And once I did, I was, like, wow, we need to get this dog out of here. There was a little bit of resistance from locals; some said things like, 'Oh, but she's the local dog, you know, she's friendly.' And I imagine I sounded a bit snappy when I pointed out to the people who had now gathered to watch this peculiar sight of me and the Thai lady lugging a chubby dog, that yes she was indeed friendly, but she was about to die here and she was obviously in chronic pain.

I showed them her terrible-looking skin. Just the small act of putting a gentle finger on her little front paw would send the sore, inflamed skin bright red. This was more serious than just an overfed dog. She was losing all her fur, it was coming away in tufts in my hands, and at that rate I could see it would all be gone in a week or two leaving her completely hairless.

Once we'd moved her out of harm's way from the passing traffic, this was without doubt a two-man job so I called in the muscles of my good mate Rod to get her someplace more safe. I couldn't lift her by myself, and that sounds harsh perhaps, but is pretty much how it felt.

For about the millionth time since I've arrived on the island, I was grateful to have Rod's assistance. The big-hearted Aussie who moved to Thailand for the more peaceful way of life, but found his hands full with the doggy scamps on the island.

Well, as soon as Rod and I had picked Cindy Crawford up and, between us, managed to get her into the box in the car to transport her, we drove her straight to the vet. We also enlisted Sybille for further back-up. We needed all the help we could get!

At surgery the local vet confirmed she weighed a whopping 46 kg (around 100 lb, or 7 st), around double of what she should have been. And, arguably, almost as much as many of the fully grown adult women here local to the island. What's more, she was riddled with parasites and a quick once-over from the vet had us estimating that Cindy Crawford was about five years old. So not an old dog despite her seeming like her best years were long behind her.

The poor thing could hardly walk 10 yards and she had trouble standing up on her little legs which must have been putting a hell of a strain on her joints not to mention her vital organs. It was crucial we had to get the weight off Cindy, with no time to hang about if we didn't want irreversible damage to her health, but it wasn't going to be easy. (I'm sure many of us can relate to having weight issues. While you might look at me and think I'm a skinny runt who has never had weight issues, I *do* know what it's like to struggle to suppress your urges. I had nothing but sympathy for this little girl and the sorry state she now had found herself in.)

The vet dished out some strong warnings though. 'Look, this dog do not do anything like put her in the sea,' we were instructed. He must have known we often like to exercise the dogs not just by running them along the beach but taking them for ocean swims, too. They tend to love the feeling of doggy paddling in the water, but this was out of the question for Cindy here.

'Do not take her on big walks,' the vet continued. 'Do not do anything that will over-exert her already strained heart, Niall.'

We were told Cindy Crawford could literally die if we went in too early and too enthusiastically with the dog's workout regime. Her inflated, bloated organs were close to failing because they were under so much pressure from carrying all that excess weight, and her blood pressure was sky high.

Finding Tina shackled and in an
extremely poor state. She broke my
heart on first sight.

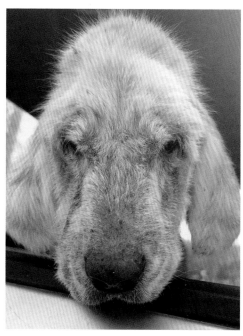

Down but not out.

Tina soon settled in and little
Rodney was always by her side.

The thing about Tina is that she absolutely
loved and trusted humans. She would
come with me on every walk. Incredible,
given what had happened to her.

I soon discovered that Tina was a very good girl. Here she is giving me her paw.

Tina with her big brothers Jumbo and Snoop.

Her favourite place was the hammock. I loved taking pictures of her when she was gently resting there.

Jumbo is a giant character. He loved the 7-Eleven and never missed a trip there. What a dog.

Jumbo and my very own Snoop at the beach. Dogs love the beach as much as humans do!

I had to have this picture in. Snoop never looked cuter. He was my very first dog and pulled me through some dark moments. There will never be another Snoop.

With my brothers and Tina. They loved her.

A stunning picture of the best girl there ever was.

My promise to Tina to build a hospital.

Looking smashing in her bandana.
She had one for every day of the week.

Cindy and Eve on their recovery
journey together.

Big Shaq: before and after.

Cindy on a health kick before we
discovered her big secret!

Buster landed on his feet.
He's now a tennis coach.

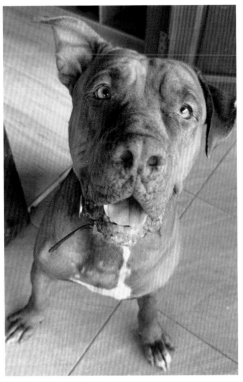

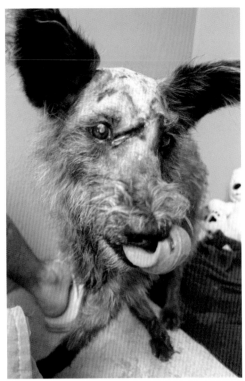

Hank the Tank, a gentle giant.

Billy, just after we found him.

My name is Niall but most people know me as that Irish guy who rescues street dogs.

Before that, though, I was an addict. When I woke up on my third day in hospital, I made a vow to myself that I would find something to live for.

I didn't have to look far. What I found in the thousands of street dogs roaming the roads and jungle tracks in Thailand was something that reminded me of me. Down but not out. Beaten but not broken. And just like me, they needed someone to love.

So that's how it started. And with every food parcel delivered on coconut-leaf trays, every dog rescued from disease, attack or injury, every special soul that I crossed paths with, I found happiness. Yet these unlikely heroes have also taught me the meaning of life.

The pack keeps growing because there are always good dogs to save.

There's al...

The first person to read *Hope* was, of course, Tina. I had to make a decision, and my decision was that dogs always come first.

I look so happy here. I wouldn't be where I am today without the love of these dogs.

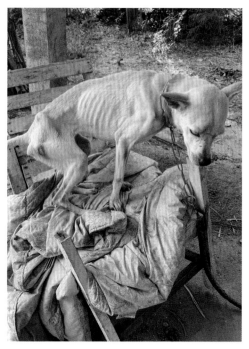

Finding Alba. Almost two years after
I found Tina, I came across Alba.
The similarities were devastating.

Rescuing Alba.
She was skin and bones.
I had to be very careful with her.

Alba takes a bite of tuna.
A big moment, but would it work?

'Alba' means sunrise or dawn – and she
loved every single one of them.

I made a vow to Alba to never miss a sunrise. Here I am, with Hank,
paying tribute to Alba, Tina, Snoop and every dog we have had to say goodbye
to, knowing that we will keep working to save as many as possible.

The vet worried that even a small shock or anything like that could kill her. So the first thing that needed to happen was to get Cindy onto the medicine, to kill the parasites to help her skin, and to lower her blood pressure and reduce cholesterol. Yes, these pills are available for dogs and all work in a similar way as they do for us humans. In most cases, dogs with high blood pressure will need to take medication for life, even if the underlying disease is treated. The goal really of any treatment with hypertension is to prevent organ damage and symptoms.

I knew it might take a while, but I was determined to get Cindy Crawford fighting fit again. She seemed like a dog that was down quite literally, for sure, but not yet out. She was so jolly and loving towards everyone.

My instinct told me that if we could just turn things around she would go on to live a long and happy life. My dream was to see her running after the moped one day in the future, along with all the other dogs, full of energy and bursting with the joys of life.

I've learned that it's important to have these dreams for the dogs, however unlikely it might seem at the time to ever achieve them. It's like that motivational saying: 'If you aim for the moon you might just reach the stars.' And anything would be better than leaving her bloated body for dead near the 7-Eleven. No animal deserves that.

★　★　★

I suppose the idea of building a hospital for dogs had been seeded in my mind before I'd even met Tina. But it was only when I had to bury her, consumed with rage at the world that animals had to put up with so much unfair treatment, that it really became a 'thing' in my head that just had to be actioned.

Now I was back on home land, it was time to really consider the best way of moving forward with the great plan and make it all become a tangible thing.

I took myself off to lay flowers on Tina's grave and have a little chat with her.

I knew the precise spot where her hospital would be built – exactly where we laid her to rest. Right from the start in my head I called it 'Tina's Hospital for Dogs Who Aren't Doing So Good'. Sounds a bit bonkers and a mouthful, but that was simply saying exactly what it was and whose honour it was being erected in. That was important to me. Tina was never 'just another dog'. She was special. They broke the mould when they made that dog. I decided that I wanted the entrance to feature a huge smiling photo of Tina.

I wanted the hospital to have the best staff, high-tech machines and most advanced medicines. Hundreds of sick and needy dogs could be treated there, just as Tina once was. She would love that.

I knew that something on this scale wouldn't happen overnight, as there would be so many logistics to consider, a lot of planning and even more funding would be needed. But as I promised to Tina, this all had to actually happen, and as quickly as humanly possible.

I'm always stupidly optimistic about how rapidly these things can be done. Initially, I thought three months might be possible. I threw myself into the research. Clearly I'm not a vet, and nor have I ever built a hospital before, but I knew I could assemble a team of experts. I tried to devise some preliminary numbers and roughly estimated the initial budget to build the centre would be between $500,000 to $1,000,000. Then the running costs would be a further $20,000 to $50,000 per month. Big scary numbers, eh?

I opened up another spreadsheet on my laptop to brainstorm ideas on how the hell I'd ever reach these figures. I knew from the start that I wanted the funding to be community-focused, so it would feel like the hospital was built not by me, but by dog lovers all over the world. The hospital would purely be for street dogs and wouldn't be focused on making money.

The early signs were that the book was selling well. I was delighted that anyone was interested, but I wouldn't have the final revenue numbers from that until the end of the year. All I was certain about was that every penny earned would go towards the hospital. I secretly hoped it might even reach six figures over the next year – that would be a good chunk towards the building works.

There was just something about Tina that made every-body want to do better. I do feel she is looking down on everything. I use her memory daily to push me on.

So many people wanted to help fundraise, but at that stage I asked them to wait until I had a detailed plan and costs. Only when the time was right and we were ready did I want to involve everyone in a community effort.

I also started thinking that wealthier individuals or companies might be interested in sponsoring some parts of the hospital: a testing machine, equipment, computers, the sort of things that we would certainly be needing. I thought if I could draw up a wishlist, people could donate and in thanks we would name things after them.

My brain was whirling away frantically looking at the spreadsheets and feeling both excited yet daunted by the months ahead. To calm myself I went and did my usual routine of driving around feeding the street dogs. It's always so grounding seeing their delight at getting our fresh dinners and receiving some affection.

I felt the sun on my back, beating down warmer than I'd felt it in months. I saw a beautiful blue butterfly flying in the wind. The sea looked the most aquamarine I'd ever seen. It was a moment of calm, like I could feel Tina's pres-ence. She was everywhere now.

CHAPTER THIRTEEN

ROCK 'N' ROLL STAR

By the autumn a good bit of land was already being cleared to prepare for Tina's Hospital so that when the time comes we could finally lay down its first foundations. So it's galling that a naughty, healthy little pup scampered into our lives through the back door – and little did we know the fate she had in store …

She was a tiny thing. Small and brown, she looked like she could be a much scruffier relative to the smart chocolate labradors that are popular in the UK. We'd started to notice her emerging from the jungle some days when we'd been on our feeding round. I guessed she was only a puppy really, *definitely (maybe)* about four months old.

Hope Avenue and the land is surrounded by dense jungle, so a young dog hanging around the edge of the sanctuary is most likely to have been put there on purpose rather than finding their own way. All the local folk know we are here, and the work we do, so I thought it likely she had probably been dumped intentionally – for us to find her and deal with her. It seems horribly callous to ditch any animal in this way but it happens, and apart from being abandoned there was no sign of any abuse from human hands, just carelessness.

It later transpired, after we'd asked around, that a family of migrant workers had been staying on the plot next to us. They had owned this dog as a puppy, but recently moved on to the next place where their work took them, and had simply left her to get on with it. It must have been confusing as hell to the pup to get left behind, but she was a cheerful little thing. I certainly wasn't going to look back after all …

There was a playful, teasing sort of vibe about her, as if she knew she was doing enough for us to notice her, yet it seemed she was too scared to come in initially. But, little by little, over the course of two or three weeks, the little pup edged in a bit closer. Some of the other dogs gave her a bit of a run for her money and there was a bit of rough and tumble if you got close to their heels or tails, but she was really very brave and ballsy. You could see in her wide brown eyes that she was terrified a lot of the time by the bigger dogs in those early days. But she never turned and ran. She was plucky and held her ground.

Each day she would come in five or ten yards more, slightly wary, and I'd see her little brown fur peeking out from the bushes. Eventually I started putting down food for her on the far side of the sanctuary and she'd gratefully hoover it up with a wagging tail. By that time we had some builders coming in to plot out where some of the foundations and things for the hospital might be, and they had started to work on clearing the overgrown land. It felt good to know it was starting to become a reality but we were still in the very early stages.

This little dog was so adorable even the burliest of the builders were charmed by her puppy dog eyes and sunny nature, and I'd noticed with a smile to myself that they'd started feeding and playing with her. That built her confidence enough to encourage her to venture in more and more towards us. She was growing less timid by the hour.

After a few more days of this little game, she took the plunge and fully invited herself in. I really respected her for this. To come in and make friends with us humans there, and make friends with the other dogs, must have been a real brave and clever thing for her to do.

She didn't have the chance to partake of anything that gave her Dutch courage, so she wasn't walking in on that first day full of beans and excited and pushing to the front of the food bowls, but she eased her way in and soon was part of the gang. I genuinely can't remember how and when we gave her the name Buttons, probably because she was simply as cute as one, but it stuck immediately.

As we saw her get her bearings into the life of the land, I used to joke with volunteers about how Buttons was the first dog who had joined us out of choice. Normally it was us going to their rescue and bringing them in. But not with this little lady.

We would talk nonsense and spin these yarns about how she had set out on the road looking for a better life and she had found it with us. Then on another day we'd joke around saying she must have mistaken us for some kind of health spa that she was checking herself into. She seemed like the kind of character who might enjoy the finer things in life. *Ooh, nice tender chicken and stewed carrots on the menu tonight, thank you, Niall, and yes please my fur might appreciate a little grooming to keep up my good looks.* A right little 'Champagne Supernova' among the other mutts.

She was great with the other dogs. Her friendly nature made her popular from the get-go with them and she rapidly became friends with old Jumbo. You can never predict which dogs will hit it off and which really won't, but that pair – despite the years between them – would wander around together like two old friends. He was the protective grandpa figure teaching her how life worked. Overall, Buttons seemed strong and healthy, but she had an old collar that was way too tight. We loosened it up a little day by day and that definitely helped her to feel more relaxed and involved. This allowed us to give her medicine for a few little ailments, get her vaccinated and then eventually sterilised as we did all the dogs.

After a while, enough time had passed that I thought even though Buttons had invited herself in, clearly no-one was looking for her and she wasn't unwell or needing any kind of long-term training or treatment. So I thought, *OK, let's get on and get you a home.* It was clear she'd make a lovely pet for someone. But who?

We went through our usual process (I'll explain how that works in a bit) and we put her up on the website for adoption. People took to her online immediately. I think it was because everyone loved her story. The idea that she was trying to create a better life for herself, and had been trekking around the jungle to find it, really appealed to people. It also probably didn't hurt that she was a lovely-looking thing.

Looking through the adoption requests is all part of the weekly admin and there's a form that potential new dog parents fill in online and then we have the results come up in a spreadsheet.

It's wonderful seeing that people are interested in offering a Thai street dog their forever home, and once we started looking there were about 30 or 40 applications that had come in, not bad, and as I scanned the names on the spreadsheet, I immediately noticed one name in particular – *Liam Gallagher.* 'Look, somebody's got the same name as Liam Gallagher,' said one of the other guys from the team who was working with me on the adoption list.

I pulled a bit of a face at him because obviously it's a very famous name ... but it's also not a particularly uncommon one. I shrugged and carried on reading.

But then, in the next column on the form which is where potential adopters fill in what they do for a living, next to occupation they had written 'singer'. Ha! As if. Come on, I thought, this is ridiculous. This was obviously my mates having a joke, or some troll with too much time on their hands winding us up with a bizarre piss-take.

I read the rest of the information in the form to see what other gags this person had come up with. But in the box for the address, there was a legitimate-looking business address, which out of curiosity I googled and found that it was connected to a Debbie Gwyther, which another little Google click told me was the name of the partner of *the* Liam Gallagher. As in the lead singer of Oasis. I suppose I wanted to believe it, as it would be hilarious to have a celebrity after one of our little dogs, but I still thought that it was more likely the work of a really, really determined troll who'd bothered to put together a more elaborate kind of hoax. It would only have taken them a bit of time researching this stuff on the internet. I couldn't see what a troll's motivation for this joke might be, but you get all sorts. I've even had marriage proposals before by some women who clearly must be a little deluded. (Hey, I'm not complaining to have 'admirers' … but you've got to accept some folk aren't all there.) So I was still a bit unsure to say the least.

There were other, general questions in the form that we ask to get a sense of the person's background and whether there might be any concerns or problems in adopting the dog, as we need to know they will have the best chance of being a good fit together. Well, the answer on this form was all about how the person travelled loads, but how they had a great set-up with other animals at home, and with friends who are huge dog lovers, and who would be able to help out with the walking and caring responsibilities.

'You know what,' I said out loud, 'I really do think this *is* the Liam Gallagher.' This is bonkers!

As exciting as this discovery was, we then had to think about what we should do. We have become quite strict about our adoption process: we interview people, do some checks and questions about the type of home the applicants have, think about the logistics of the dog reaching their new home, that kind of thing. So, on the one hand we were saying, 'OK, let's keep calm and stick with our process,' and on the other hand we were joking, 'Can we really ask Liam Gallagher to turn up to one of our little Zoom interviews about housing a dog?!' In the end we talked it out, with quite a lot of laughing and making intended and unintended puns, and decided that, yes, we had to stick with our usual adoption process. Riches and fame aside, we couldn't let a superstar singer off the hook with the stringent measures we'd carefully put in place here.

So, that's precisely how we found ourselves a week later on a video call with the Oasis star himself. I won't lie, I was a bit nervous. I should have just shut it all out and thought, *All we're doing is applying our usual day to day work*, but instead my mind was racing with lots of thoughts about what would and would not be appropriate to ask and say.

Throughout my life I'd come across famous people but this was different. Still I suppose you could argue that I shouldn't have been the least bit thrown by seeing a famous face pop up on my laptop screen as I sat in my little shipping container office. But, you know what? I still was a bit. I mean, come on, it was Liam Gallagher!

I'd like to think that he needs no introduction, but if you're looking for one, well he is a rock and roll star.

I was definitely an Oasis fan at that time, and had actually seen them live a few times, but I don't think it's an exaggeration to say nearly everybody of my age from the UK and Ireland is, in some way, influenced by the band. We've all shouted the words to 'Wonderwall' at a party (or fallen in love listening to it) or had our spirits lifted by the soaring chorus of 'Live Forever'. Liam and Noel Gallagher were the northern brothers who were brash, cocky and knew they were talented. Noel was often touted as the thinking one who was funny enough to do stand-up, while Liam was the wild child frontman, often wearing John Lennon-style round sunglasses and giving interviewers an earful.

And now, here I was, about to interview one of them about the possibility of adopting one of our dogs …

So we clicked 'Join Meeting' and there, after a short pause for the video to go live on Zoom, was Liam

Gallagher looking brilliant and exactly like you would expect Liam Gallagher to look. A bit shaggy haired, unshaven, I think he even had one of his classic green shirts on, sipping tea from a cup.

'I hope you're OK after Tina, we loved that dog,' were the first words from Liam and it stopped me in my tracks. Here was a famous singer asking me about Tina. That's the sort of effect she had on people. I brushed it off and said everything was fine and I missed her and thanks, but I knew then. Liam and Debbie were genuine dog lovers, and their intentions were genuine about Buttons too. I gave a huge sigh of relief and continued the interview.

Although his appearance was precisely like you would expect, in person he seemed so mellow and relaxed, not like the tough-talking, sweary singer I'd always seen on TV. They were immediately very friendly, and I started asking all our usual research questions.

Over the months we've been finding new homes for the dogs, the majority of applicants have been from women. I'm not saying there are more female dog lovers than male ones, but perhaps they're just more motivated to get things done. Or more organised or something (yes, hugely stereotyping here, I'm sorry). Certainly when there is a family or couple applying for dogs it's often the female who leads things and the men go along with it. So to be honest I was expecting Debbie to do most of the talking in our virtual meeting. I had convinced myself that this would be the case here, with Liam mostly a bystander sitting next to the real boss of the situation.

But this wasn't the case with Liam. He was absolutely not just appeasing his dog-loving partner but was massively and genuinely enthusiastic.

Like most conversations with new people, the first exchanges were friendly and straight, but after about five minutes, Liam started talking about some of the other big characters we have at the land and whose stories he was following online, and it was just amazing. 'That Jumbo is a bit of a mad one, in't he? Always going over to the convenience store,' and, 'Whacker was great, going over to Scotland.' He knew all about McMuffin's cancer journey too. It was so surreal, having this megastar tell us that they were a fan of what we did, and which of the Happy Doggos made him laugh. Once we'd all relaxed it was just like chatting to mates.

It was clear what conscientious animal lovers they were. Liam and Debbie had even been looking at a few of the different dogs we had put up for adoption in the past, but it seemed to me they had always talked themselves out of it, because it hadn't felt like the right time for them. Liam had been recording, or they had had to spend time in LA and stuff like that. I was impressed that they'd realised that wouldn't be great for a new dog settling in and hadn't just acted on a whim and then farmed out the caring duties (which they clearly could have afforded to). Instead, they'd waited until the time was right to welcome in a new family member. And that time was now. And little Buttons would be the perfect fit.

I came off the Zoom having completed the full interview process. There were no shortcuts taken even for these VIPs, because in my mind the dogs are the only real VIPs and the ones that really matter the most. But I felt confident that Liam and Debbie would be excellent carers.

As I put food out for little Buttons that evening I gave her a lot of cuddles and told her she'd be needing her passport and some warmer clothes for England. 'You've got a new mummy and daddy,' I grinned as she wagged her tail. 'And they are going to love you to bits, little one.'

The timing was such that I was due back to Europe again to do some more promotion work and it made sense to take Buttons on that long journey with me.

There is a big preamble to each journey though. It takes about four months to complete all the paperwork and testing required for a dog to travel to another country. With brave little Buttons I travelled to Bangkok initially, and from there flew to Europe. My lovely dad met us, and then we took Buttons across to the UK in the Channel Tunnel and then finally up to London. Buttons was amazing and took all of this transporting in her stride. When we arrived she was clearly feeling a lot fresher than I was.

TINA

I was relieved to be finally arriving at Liam Gallagher's smart front door in London, however unreal it felt. Whenever I have delivered dogs to new owners outside of Thailand before, there is always a little reflective moment when I realise how bizarre it is to be dropping off an animal who was given up for dead next to a building site or on a dirt road or something. That feeling was massively amplified with Buttons and Liam; here was a dog who'd been in the middle of the jungle, half the world away, and now there I was delivering her to what I knew was going to be a life of Riley.

When we introduced Buttons to Liam, Debbie and, perhaps more importantly, their two cats, everything went so well. We had a cup of tea and watched on as Buttons settled in instantly, and within only a few minutes it was like she had lived there forever and they were all (including the cats!) one newly formed happy family.

It's been so wonderful to see what has happened since. They're besotted with Buttons. Truly, they have fallen head over heels in love with that dog and nothing makes me happier or prouder of the little girl. For obvious reasons, Liam and Debbie don't have major social media presences, but they send me photos and then I'll share the odd one but I check they're OK with that first. People love knowing what happens next to the dogs we take in. But I'm mindful to protect privacy. Buttons wouldn't give a hoot – she's a right little show-off – but I'm careful not to show the outside of their house or their location and compromise them in any way.

When they do share pictures of Buttons, I have to laugh. One day she's in a big country house or some chic part of London. The next week she's wolfing from her bowl and it's filled with steak. The next time, she is lying in bed with an era-defining rock star. After that, this rock star is literally serenading her, singing songs to Buttons. She has just landed on her feet, and it fits perfectly with all those silly stories we used to spin when we first met her about her seeking out our shelter looking for a better life.

Liam and Debbie have become wonderful supporters of what we do. They donated the globe that Liam used on one of his latest tours towards raising funds for Tina's Hospital. A fitting donation as it really did mean the world to me that they were helping to celebrate Tina in some way.

We have adopted so many dogs now that it seems a bit mean to them to single out Buttons, but to have a dog loved as much as she is, in a home with the Oasis frontman, who has become a huge supporter of what we do here at Happy Doggo, has been too incredible not to share.

It felt like a ringing and star-sprinkled endorsement of what we do. I think for a lot of people with a bit more money, there is a big temptation to go out and buy an expensive dog with a long breeding history. So having

Liam Gallagher adopting a dog from a shelter sends out a great message.

Having said that, although being associated with celebrity and all that it brings is great, the most important thing, I think, is to bring it back to Buttons just a little lost puppy in search of a home to call her own.

Also, I did joke at the time, 'Maybe Buttons will help get the band back together.' So I'm putting it all down to Buttons being the kind, loving soul that she is, healing the rifts and giving the world the gift of an Oasis reunion. And if you're reading this, Liam, give Buttons a cuddle from me.

CHAPTER FOURTEEN

NIALL GOES TO HOLLYWOOD

It turned out to be a super-busy few weeks that October, because no sooner had I returned from the second trip taking little Buttons to her new mum and dad in London, I felt like I was packing up bags once again to set off to America.

It seems mad – but brilliant – that there are people in the USA who follow the lives of the Thai dogs on Insta and Twitter. So it was decided that I'd make a trip to the States to try and do some publicity there, too. 'Cracking America' felt like something rock bands do, so it felt hilarious that little me was having a minor but enthusiastic attempt.

It is a big old place, and the visit was another whirlwind trip where I'd tried to cram in as much as physically possible in just a few days. The walks in Tina's name had been such an unexpected and heart-warming success in the UK, I held three similar ones on the other side of the pond.

In Los Angeles, the first stopover, I did the walk at the stunning Griffith Park, which for any movie buffs is where

La La Land was filmed. You might remember the scene where Emma Stone and Ryan Gosling are tap dancing together on a street on Mount Hollywood in Griffith Park? Well, that's where me and lots of lovely American dogs (and their equally lovely humans) all congregated. And it was as joyful as the UK ones had been, albeit with fewer people this time. The park also boasts the best vantage point for observing the world-famous Hollywood sign (and so of course I made sure to get a snap of me in front of that for posterity).

I also had another reason to call in via LA (perhaps the biggest reason if I'm honest) and that was to check up on little Brad Pitt. The month before, he'd finally got his own forever home in America, and I was dying to see him and how he was settling into his new life.

I'd first met him the year before, and at first glance he'd looked like a big, fluffy dog. It wasn't until I pulled in to give him a treat one day when I realised it wasn't just nice, fluffy fur – it was grossly matted, as he'd picked up parts of foliage along the way which was getting caught up in the poor thing's own toilet matter. Not nice for anyone.

When I finally managed to catch him and sedate him I could tackle the grooming with a pair of clippers which was no small task. But once I did it was incredibly satisfying removing all that manky fur the poor lad had been carrying around. And boy did he look like a completely different dog afterwards. I shared the before and afters on social media and people were in disbelief. 'That's not the same dog!' they all commented on the post. Even friends who'd seen him in real life couldn't believe the transformation. I had to tell them all to look at his nose to see that it really was the same little mutt, just with an incredible 'glow-up'.

Once he'd got his cool new image it became clear that Brad was such a friendly, affectionate dog he'd make a wonderful pet for someone. I never found out his back-story, but it seems likely he was abandoned by someone who'd originally wanted a cute, fluffy dog, but then didn't bother to care for him. What was quite clear to me was that he wasn't meant for the streets, he wasn't one of the typical animals we see round here. And he was better off being safely adopted.

People online had fallen in love with him, and luckily the perfect match ended up being in California. He now has two humans and two cat friends. I thought it was brilliantly fitting that Brad Pitt the dog would be going to America – and not far from Hollywood. You couldn't make that story up really. It was great to know it had all turned out for the best for him.

Two days later, I found myself doing another walk, this time at Crissy Field in the beautiful city of San Francisco. It's a truly stunning place to dog walk as there's amazing views of the Bay and the world-famous Golden Gate Bridge. I'm told that some parts of *Mrs Doubtfire* starring Robin Williams were filmed here.

Then in another two days after that, I was in the Big Apple, and of course any walk taking place in New York just had to held in the city's famous Central Park. If I listed all the films that have used Central Park for a scene or two it would take up too much space – it's literally the most filmed location in the world and larger than the country of Monaco. It's even got 10,000 benches, so there were plenty of options for those walkers who wanted a little rest that day.

I think about 500 New Yorkers turned up for that one, all bringing their four-legged friends and typically high spirits. It was truly wonderful, and the local media came out to film some coverage of the event.

Everything in America is just supersized, I can never get my head round it all, and it felt like a million miles away from the life I lead in Thailand. It was a worthwhile trip, but it was totally exhausting if I'm honest too. On the UK trip I was running on pure adrenaline and well wishes, but I perhaps had bitten off more than I could chew with the American one.

On the plane I looked out the window and thought about the fact we were flying over entire countries and it made me think about all the dogs down there and all the help they'd need. The scale of the issue globally is incredibly daunting, I knew how hard it was just fixing one tiny part of Thailand. I felt anxiety rising and a negative thought brewing in my mind: *What's the point in trying? This is too big to take on.*

When these unhelpful thoughts creep in, I try to shut them down as fast as I can. And remember how lucky I am to have so many people supporting me. I never want to let the dogs down, but I also don't want to let everybody who follows along on this journey down either. I know I am so blessed to get to do this, but you can't help having little wobbles along the way.

By the time I got back to Koh Samui I'd come down with the flu. I think I'd overdone it basically and picked up a bug on the aeroplane or from the aircon on board. So with that, and along with the jet lag, I definitely wasn't feeling at my best for a couple of weeks.

But the plans for the hospital were ticking along nicely. I'd realised by then that my original hope to have it up and running in three months was crazily naive. I then decided six months would be realistic because there were all sorts of things I had no idea about, that would all take time and which I couldn't have speeded up, however much I'd wanted to. Practical stuff such as building permissions and the licences and legalities. Everything needed to be in correct order as there was no way I would be allowing this venture to fail. There also needed to be an official charter and operational procedures decided, like who gets treated, how to deal with long-term stays, how to manage free care, and so on.

Essentially, all the work that would be taking place in

Tina's Hospital was all happening anyway, but having a physical place to centre all the work made so much sense – and would save resources in the long term.

We were already heavily upscaling the crucial sterilising programme now, in multiple locations, and there were sick puppies and multiple dogs at different vets. We were spending between $2,000 to $5,000 a month on small but crucial life-saving operations but the number of dogs I could help now was limited by costs, vet space, transport and the lack of certain medical machines on the island.

Tina's Hospital would be able to fix all that and I kept my iron-clad promise to her at the front of my mind at all times. I even turned her pictures into my computer screen saver as a constant reminder of what the big picture was when it felt like I'd taken on more than I could handle with the hospital build.

On one side was a photo of Tina on the day she arrived, broken and with her bones showing … and on the other side of the screen was Tina looking her fabulous best in her finest bandana. Every time I glanced at my screen it really drove me on. It also served as a reminder to me when I was feeling overstretched and pushing myself too hard, that Tina the golden retriever's transformation took many months. Good things take time and patience, I reminded myself. The hospital would be achieved, just not overnight.

★   ★   ★

Meanwhile Cindy Crawford was keeping us busy. The first steps to recovery can be the hardest, and remember that Cindy was so ill when she arrived we were advised against even taking her for a swim at the beach as she might have a heart attack. She was so big that we couldn't even tie one of our bandanas around her neck.

It took us about three weeks to diagnose that Cindy wasn't just naturally greedy, she also actually suffered a thyroid problem. Untreated thyroid issues were making her gain weight and it had become almost impossible to shift. Once we had got the right medication though, and were able to slip a daily pill into her food to solve that issue, Cindy started losing a little bit of weight. And that medication, coupled with the diet we'd devised, slowly started having the desired effect. She'll have to take the tablets for life, but it entirely changed her outlook.

After seven weeks in our care she'd shed 5 kg (about 11.5 lb) and Cindy had begun acting like a completely different dog. Before, it was as if she'd given up on life and was done mentally and physically. Now, she had more energy and had started following us humans everywhere. It was seriously cute.

Her diet was tough though. Essentially it involved making sure she always ate just small portions. She was given low-fat food, lean bits of chicken and things like that, which admittedly she sort of hated. In fairness to her, however, she did eat it, if a little begrudgingly. I imagine it's like the equivalent of eating salads all the time for us humans – you might do it to try and look a bit better after a blowout at Christmas, or before a holiday to get trim, but it's not exactly fun. And soon you start salivating at the smell of bacon or freshly baked bread.

But her diet plan, which the vet helped devise, had to be quite severe initially to get those excess kilos down and take some strain off her legs and heart. We made sure she always had lots of water to keep her hydrated, as well as to try and stop her eating when she might actually just be thirsty.

She looked huge for weeks, almost inflated, I used to joke (affectionately). She'd waddle about, like a huge potato with four little sorts of toothpicks for legs.

And then as the weight started dropping – a few pounds a week – we were able to give her all the nutritious food needed to make her skin as healthy as possible. Her fur had literally been coming away in great clumps and tufts in my hands at first, so it was wonderful to see that stopping and her bald spots gradually growing back.

Once I'd shared Cindy's story on social media, I think many people really related to the plucky little dog's heroic weight battle. Over the weeks it became clear to everyone that here was an unbelievably friendly character with such a gentle spirit. But as she grew in confidence it was soon like she owned the place.

She naturally had a motherly way about her, or the kind of auntie everyone loves. All the other dogs on the land adored her. No other dog picked on her or growled at her. She never had to find her place in the pack or anything like that, which is quite common when we bring in new animals as the others don't always love sharing the attention. When they've waited so long in their lives to get any, you can hardly blame them really.

But although she was popular and born to be sociable, I had to make her a little separate area in the office on the land, because it was crucial that Cindy didn't hoover up anyone else's leftovers.

Every week we'd weigh her, and any pounds and kilos lost would be a little celebration for everyone following her progress. I imagine it's like those Weight Watchers group meetings when people all stand around clapping if someone has reached a goal that week or seen an improvement. There was so much support for her.

And I was personally so excited about her progress. Sometimes I couldn't resist secretly getting her onto the scales every two days, just because I was so stupidly pleased with her. I was jubilant whenever Cindy had shed anything – and couldn't help lavishing her with cuddles and hugs. I was so proud of my girl.

A few more weeks into her little journey though, and Cindy's weight loss mysteriously plateaued. Why? I had to investigate. At the start, people were very good at sticking to the diet. It was crucial to prevent her from having a heart attack. But then, once Cindy had lost a bit of weight and her life seemed less at risk, I started rewarding her with a treat. Only because her diet was so tough and I felt sorry for her.

There are always treats kept on the land. I like to give one to every dog before bed along with a cuddle and a kiss on their furry snouts so they know they are loved. It's usually little pieces of beef jerky and things like that. We also have sausages on hand if we want to hide medicine in them to give to tricky dogs. Treats are useful, and with Cindy being such a cute, adorable slimmer, I didn't think it would matter so much. What harm could one treat do?!

After several weigh-in meetings in a row where I'd be left scratching my head in confusion saying, 'Hmm, why is Cindy's weight not going down?' and then listening to us all argue about different foods and the like that might have been to blame.

Something was going on. I knew that I was sneaking her a treat but surely I was the only one. 'Has anyone been giving Cindy any extra treats by any chance?' I asked the group of volunteers, looking around the room at six people all looking slightly sheepish and innocently shaking their heads. No one said anything. That's when the penny dropped. I wasn't the only one giving Cindy treats – we were all doing it on the sly. Busted!

It became quite a comedy moment really, and eventually we all agreed to put our hand up if we had ever slipped up. Sure enough, all seven of us in the room owned up and apologised. We all promised to be stricter for Cindy's own sake. Sometimes you have to be cruel to be kind as they say. And none of us had been able to resist giving in to Cindy's little begging eyes and salivating mouth.

It was a long, hard slog getting that dog down to a regular, healthy weight, and it really taught me that for anybody trying to lose weight – or in fact trying to achieve anything at all in life – the thing that is most needed is *consistency*.

With the diet, but also with the gentle exercise, from baby walks to beach runs eventually, Cindy impressed us all by showing up and doing her daily steps.

As she grew in energy it meant the walks could be a little longer each time.

It absolutely made my heart sing when, after about five months, she spontaneously broke into a run on the beach one day. We had actually been trying to get her weighed and get her meds down her, but she had other plans and joyfully darted off. I couldn't help breaking into a run myself because I was so happy that Cindy was now embracing her new physique and seemed so delighted to have got a second chance. She'd gone from having given up on the street, to now being able to run on the sand.

Cindy Crawford really had got the 'glow-up' I'd always hoped she would, befitting her supermodel namesake. Her character was so vivacious, and she'd started to look just as bubbly and vibrant as her little personality clearly was.

In total it took nine months from her original rescue for Cindy Crawford to have got down to 29 kg (having lost 14 kg – good effort, girl). She still had a little to go, but she'd added years to her life and looked incredible, not just from her impressive weight loss, but with her glossy, thick white fur that now began to grow back and that big radiant smile of hers. I have a lovely photo of her looking out to sea with her paws crossed, wearing a watermelon bandana. She really does sum up everything we do at Happy Doggo.

Funnily enough the real life Cindy Crawford, the famous supermodel, found out about our four-legged friend, and apparently thought it was hilarious they shared the same name. It's so funny because Jennifer Anniston, the *Friends* actress, also follows us on Instagram and 'likes' some of the videos and posts we make (no doubt slightly amused that we named a dog after her ex-hubby Brad Pitt!).

There are many of other celebrities who follow us which I continue to find equal parts amusing and surreal. But the one famous fan that really blew my mind was Ronnie O'Sullivan, the snooker-playing legend, because I'd long looked up to him. Ronnie suffers from depression like me, and was a real hero of mine for a long time (and still is). In fact, in the depths of my depression back in the desperate drinking days I once even wrote to Ronnie telling him how bad I was feeling. So I was chuffed to bits when he sent me a video message about the dogs and I can see he follows their journeys online.

Sometimes I have to pinch myself because life takes so many surreal little turns.

CHAPTER FIFTEEN

WHEN WE SLAM DUNKED A NASTY TUMOUR

Many dogs come and go at the land, with some only need-ing a quick helping hand to get them back on their feet. But we meet a lot more animals than I could ever post about online, and while I shouldn't admit it I do sometimes have secret favourite dogs. Shaq was someone who defi-nitely became a bit special to me because his problem was unusually grisly. And that animal just showed such remark-able resilience.

I first heard about Shaq when a tourist sent a photo to me. I've had to learn how to prioritise these canine emergencies, almost like operating a triage system in emergency departments in hospitals. It's a case of catego-rising each problem into urgent, and not so urgent, and working through things from there. The day we got sent Shaq's photo, the team was frantically busy, there was loads of stuff going on and free time was short. But, just like in Tina's case, the image was so shocking it was one of those moments when you immediately down tools. I knew I had to find the time to drive down and see what was going on.

A local had spotted him by the roadside and been horri-fied by the enormous – and I really do mean *vast* – growth on the right side of his neck. Whatever the hell it was, it needed urgent attention, and this wasn't something I'd come across in any other dog rescue.

This massive growth was quite grotesque and the size was shocking; it looked almost like a basketball. I named him Shaq, after the seven-foot tall American basketball legend Shaquille O'Neal who played for the Orlando Magic. He was my all-time favourite basketball player and this boy was going to need a lot of magic. Anyway, back to the problem at hand. *What the hell happened here?* I muttered, wincing at the image on my phone.

I immediately rang Rod, who else, and explained we needed to find this dog straightaway. Shaq was living near a house, the tourist had said, but the poor fella clearly wasn't being looked after. Rod and I got to the right area as the tourist had explained, and then split up while we tried to find him. I really didn't know what to expect in the flesh – the gruesome photo was bad enough.

In fact, as I spotted him lumbering up in the distance, it seemed even worse in real life. *Wow, how big is that thing?* I couldn't imagine how long it had been growing there, and hated to think how uncomfortable it must have been for him lugging it around 24/7. The weight of it had stretched the poor thing's skin to the extent it was hanging down and flapping around his neck.

Over the past two years we have seen lots of horrific injuries, including King Whacker, the dog who'd been axed in the head (I know, *how could you?*), or even just as recent as the other day when we cut a tight chain from a dog's neck. There's no rhyme or reason for some of the stuff people put dogs through.

It was clear that Shaq's problem was unlikely to have been caused by abuse, or a car injury or parasites, but I had never seen something that size before. There's no room for being squeamish with this work. In the same way that Rod and I rescued little McMuffin the year before, whose rotting flesh made us both gag the first time we picked her up, you just had to toughen up. For however much it hurt my eyes looking at Shaq, this poor fella was living with it.

Unsurprisingly, as I tried to approach him, Shaq came at me very aggressively, baring his teeth. He was obviously in a world of pain. The growth didn't just look like a basketball, it seemed to weigh about as much as one, with gravity dragging his whole face down. My first instinct told me it was a nasty tumour. I imagined that I'd take this dog to the vet, they'd say it was cancer and that there was nothing they could do, and then I'd have to steel myself for this dog living out the rest of his life in misery.

I knew it wasn't fair to let him exist in this state, so we softened him up with a few sausages and got him into one of our transport boxes and drove him to the vet. She too let out a scream at the sight and size of the thing. Once we'd calmed Shaq with sedatives, she was able to gently insert a needle into the growth and managed to drain off a bit of watery fluid. This reduced the size by about 10 per cent, so not a lot. And in a way all that served to do was make us look at the still almighty mass and think, *My God, what are we going to do here?*

The vet had explained that she couldn't deal with this tumour; it was simply too big. I wanted a second opinion though as I didn't feel ready to write him off just yet. So we took Shaq to a bigger animal hospital where they looked at him and they said, 'Let's try and drain it.' We got him up on the table and drained some more fluid which they said that they would need to send it away for tests. Whatever these showed, we were warned, the team probably were not going to be able to operate, because the mass was made up of all sorts of things like blood vessels, skin, muscles and fluid and was too close to some very serious structures in the neck.

It wasn't looking good for the dog, yet we took him back to the land so we could treat the simple things we're now used to dealing with – the ticks and fleas and getting a meal in his tummy.

In the meantime, the samples had to be sent to Bangkok for analysis. After about four or five days, the results came back. To my surprise, there was good news – the growth wasn't cancer after all, and there was actually nothing nasty in there. The vets said that Shaq could have a decent shot at survival *if* they could somehow manage to successfully cut this thing out, but as we could literally see it growing by day, like some terrifying alien in a movie, it all felt very precarious.

Several vets we tried didn't want to go near the operation as it was too risky. Taking all the medical information into account, they all said, 'No chance. He won't make it.' Now obviously this is right: if you don't think that a dog will make it through the surgery with his life intact, you shouldn't go down that road. But I just couldn't give up on him once I knew it wasn't terminal.

Shaq had some fight in him, I could see that. He was a strong dog who deserved a chance. His early aggression, I guessed, was only because he was in pain. Eventually, we found a highly skilled specialist vet who agreed – while making no promises – that he'd take Shaq's case on.

After three years of dealing with vets now, I have learned that they rarely give you a percentage of success or failure: they're reluctant to over-promise and give false hope. But in lieu of that professional opinion, I've now become pretty good at coming up with my own guesstimates, and I reckoned we were going into the operation with maybe just a 20 to 30 per cent chance of Shaq pulling through. This wasn't about just draining more fluid, it would involve big incisions into and around his neck, needing to skilfully avoid all the major veins, arteries, muscles and breathing tubes that flow through there. Making sure his tongue remained intact was another worry. It was all well and good taking the tumour off, but if we were then left with a dog who couldn't feed himself we'd have another awful problem. Despite these considerable risks, I couldn't shake my gut feeling that this dog had a chance at life.

The next step was complicated because we wanted to fix Shaq and get him pain free as soon as the vet had time to operate. But because the dog also had severe anaemia and tick fever in his blood, he would not have survived the operation had it happened immediately – there would be a high chance of him bleeding to death on the operating table during any surgery.

So it was a case of being patient – the vets told us it would need three weeks to build up Shaq's strength – get medicines into him and somehow get him fit for the big operation.

We had to concentrate on the initial challenge of getting Shaq physically fit. The mass on his neck had to be drained as much as possible daily just to stop it further expanding.

It was heartbreaking to watch such a naturally proud animal be so physically and mentally burdened by his bizarre condition. Despite his suffering though, there was a spark in his dark eyes that told me he still had the will to fight. *Don't give up on me yet, Niall*, he seemed to say.

I'd grown protective of this little fighter – he was a street dog through and through. He had been in battles, he was rough looking and streetwise, but that meant he did not settle in well at all on the land.

Each dog we bring into Happy Doggo Land is allocated their own little kennel; we make it so nice for them with blankets and even soft toys for comfort, I like to call them 'VIP suites'. But Shaq wasn't aware that he was getting any special treatment. He just wasn't used to being enclosed, even if it was for all the right reasons like keeping him safe and trying to make him better.

So instinctively he tried to chew his way through the kennel. He was even strong enough that we had to reinforce the structure with bricks, which we'd never had to do with a dog before or since.

He was pacing around in his kennel, almost like a prisoner plotting an escape. His obvious uneasiness made us all uneasy too, and I just wasn't at all sure if we were doing the right thing to be honest. Was this actually better for Shaq to have us interfering like this, and were we trying to play God instead of letting nature take her course?

But as those days of trying to get him operation-fit ticked along, we began to see a real change in the dog's demeanour on the land. After about a week with us he was eating well and seemed more relaxed. He wasn't exactly offering his paw to me, but he knew me and no longer bared his teeth when I came near him.

I think he realised that we were actually there to help him. One of the things I have really learned is that you can always see a moment where the dog truly relaxes and thinks, 'OK, some of my problems are starting to go away. These people are nice. This isn't my territory, but I'm OK.' It's a beautiful moment of trust and I'll never take that for granted.

It was after seeing these subtle but significant changes taking place that I really began to think there was a good chance that he might actually survive this. And then I was so desperately willing him on. There was still a massive risk from such major surgery, and he'd become so improved by receiving some love and simple treatment that it would really be difficult to accept if he then died during the operation. I felt like I had a dog's life in my hands.

It was hard to sleep for those nights. I'd get into bed after a long day with the other dogs, or dealing with the ever growing admin for the hospital build, and would find myself tossing and turning and having the odd nightmare about a growth in my neck that looked like poor Shaq's.

In the end, the eternal optimist in me decided – let's try the operation and give him a chance.

By the time the day came for Shaq to set off, I truly loved him. In those three weeks when I'd built him up physically, we'd built up a deep connection and understanding. I was so worried as I watched him go into the operating room, I looked into his dark eyes before he went under, and he looked right back at me, holding my eye contact and never blinking. I smiled at him. *You're going to be OK, Shaq*, I whispered in his good ear. I had no idea if it was true, but I wanted him to see the last face before he went under as someone who loved him and was willing him on.

I was a wreck during that four-hour operation, pacing up and down a lot and drinking coffee as I checked my phone and tried to get on with the hospital plans and finding architects.

When he was finally out – alive and breathing – I was so thrilled, but I soon realised that waiting for Shaq to come out of the operating room was only just the beginning. The operating team took pictures of the two massive globes of stuff they removed. They were huge and spherical and a dark red colour like wine. It really was a perfect example of the old phrase 'better out than in'.

But it wasn't an easy journey for the dog.

When he came around from the anaesthetic, he was in so much pain, and had been through such a traumatic surgery, that he was making this terrible sound. It was a haunting mixture of crying and moaning, and just a deep, deep sadness noise. I've never seen a dog with such a visceral reaction to an operation. It was obvious that the procedure had taken so much out of him that there was going to be a long and hard period of recovery.

Driving him back with us was initially euphoric that he'd actually made it through the op and was still with us, but the heartbreaking noises he was making were just gut wrenching. We were all in tears as we drove away while listening to his utter anguish.

I knew I needed to keep a close eye on him so we brought him back to my place. He was cold, he was shaken, and he was still making those god awful noises. I felt terrible that day, thinking that although Shaq had made it through the operation, he was going to die anyway. This felt like the worst possible outcome and I was to blame really by thinking we should do it. Having him there in the spare room of my house, wondering if he was going to take his next breath, was horrendous. Obviously, in the UK there would be post-operative care from the vet, but here on tropical islands, once the operation was done, then it fell to me to look after Shaq.

That first night felt very long. I spent most of the time just watching him and hoping that he would make it. He was in a bad way, a really bad way, for about two days. I sat with him throughout this period asking myself, *Is he going to make it?* We had to frequently change his bandages and nurse him with both kindness and medical rigour.

Over the next couple of days, as he steadily improved we were able to take him out on his first walk. We didn't overdo it, it was just for a short time to get a little bit of fresh air really. I definitely thought, *He's gonna make it!* and allowed myself to feel quite upbeat.

But then he took a turn for the worse. His jaw swelled up, a bit like one of those old cartoons of people when they have their wisdom teeth out, all puffed up with a big white bandage wrapped around his whole head. His face became so big it would have been comical if it wasn't clear he was in a lot of pain, and the knock-on effect was that the stitches wouldn't close.

The weather outside became really bad and Shaq's health seemed to mirror that. He was there in his bed and we were all very worried. All of a sudden, with no warning, his face exploded. It wasn't healing. It looked almost like he'd been punched in the face repeatedly; his main wounds started turning black, blue, red and purple and becoming infected. It was so worrying I immediately assumed he wasn't going to make it. This creeping unease spread through us all and then was made even worse when we saw how worried the vets were. Sybille was really concerned too – from her experience with human patients she didn't like the look of things.

It transpired that although the main procedure had been a success, he had to go back for a second operation to clean things up and remove some swelling and early scar tissue. We had been warned that this might be necessary, but the first one was so stressful for him that I was really worried to be honest. Luckily, this second trip turned out to be a much smaller operation, and less painful and stressful for him.

With the two procedures over, Shaq's recovery could begin. This was the moment when I fully understood how life-changing Tina's Hospital would be for emergency situations like this. Not only that, but having a place to treat sick dogs quickly and with the correct tools seems absolutely necessary. I think it took about two to three weeks for Shaq to get better.

Watching him suffering through those times was terrible, but slowly and surely he came around and the relief was huge. His smile began to return and that gave us all hope. He was full of energy and he seemed genuinely grateful. He understood that we were helping him and nursing him to full fitness.

The swelling eventually went down. His stitches were removed, and more than any of the physical things, he just came alive again. He was barking at dogs. He was trying to manoeuvre his way into places where he could get more treats. In short, he was just like I had always hoped he would be. Soon, the stitches were clean, the whole lump was gone and there was some real pep back in his step.

It was such a rollercoaster, but by the end Shaq was looking great. When he was finally back to full health and the scars had faded, I even put him in Tina's old bandana, which I thought was very fitting. I think Tina would have loved to see him wearing that bandana, because she knew the true meaning of fight and illness. She would have loved to see Shaq's recovery, and his return, and appreciating all the life he had left to live.

It was such fun to take a fully recovered Shaq for a bit of a play together, to explore places with him and go for walks. He and I got up to all sorts. I gave him his first-ever ice cream at the beach. Watching him enjoy that simple pleasure, feeling the sand under his paws and the cool breeze on his face, was a moment of pure joy. He looked so happy and carefree now he was no longer carrying the weight of the world around his poor neck.

I would love to be inside his head to see what he is thinking now with his newfound lightness.

Shaq is proof that you should never give up in life. There were so many moments where we didn't think he'd make it. His transformation to date is nothing short of miraculous. Comebacks are always possible. Shaq's story is a testament to the power of love, care and never giving up. He has shown us all that no matter how dire the circumstances there is always hope. His journey from the streets to the beach, from despair to joy, is a story that will inspire us forever. Shaq is not just a survivor; he's a beacon of hope and a reminder that every life is worth fighting for. Sometimes it can be just as important to save one life as it is to save thousands.

CHAPTER SIXTEEN

CHARITY BEGINS AT HOME

'Congratulations, Niall, Happy Doggo is officially a registered charity!' came the happy news from Lindsay as I took the call that November morning. 'Are you serious? What about the US?' I asked tripping over my words, not believing a word.

'Oh yes, I forgot. The US too, it's all there, check your email!' she bellowed down the phone.

It had been such an onerous thing for us to go through. This really was a huge milestone for us.

It's a long and stringent procedure to go through because there are (quite rightly) so many rules in place to make sure no-one is using the charity to commit fraud. Everyone who donates to any kind of charity naturally needs to be safe in the knowledge that their cash will be put towards the cause they're choosing to support, and not some dodgy person writing themselves fat cheques.

Not everyone who applies for charity status gets it; in the UK around 20 to 30 per cent of applications are turned down. You need to go through a very thorough process, clearly laying out on paper all the intentions of the charity, what it will cost and who it will help. You need a specific goal and to be able to express that and back it up. Of course making sure it's all legally compliant is essential. And that's what we did. Determined to get it right, I wanted to give it the best chance.

Happy Doggo is a charity that focuses on grant giving, which means we help fund people who sterilise dogs. It's worth repeating, this is the most important thing there is to effectively stop the cycle of unwanted dogs. So, if there are charities out there or other organisations who want to start sterilising dogs, we now have the power to be able to step in and help them with that.

My vision has been crystal clear from the start about what was needed (neutering and spaying) and I've learned along the way the most efficient way of getting the operations safely done. So at least that part was fairly straightforward to explain.

But none of the nitty-gritty official paperwork stuff was my forte to be honest. It needed to be done though, and properly done, so I found a brilliant lady to deal with this task. Lindsay is our Head of Operations at Happy Doggo and she's been a key player for the past two years making everything work smoothly. She first reached out to me during a challenging period when I needed help, initially volunteering her time. Then she had a part-time role, and she eventually joined us full-time and quite frankly now we couldn't manage without her.

She keeps everything running seamlessly and making sure we meet all legal requirements and maintain compliance which is crucial for such a large charity.

I always get far too much credit for the work I do with the dogs when it really is a team effort.

There's also Anna, our Chief Financial Officer, who became the 'mum' of one of our original rescue dogs Moritz. She's been a vast help for scaling up the charity globally as she used to work for huge companies with tens of thousands of staff so can deal with the financial side of things. And then there's Zoe, our wonderful adoption coordinator who works behind the scenes trying to match up dogs to their forever homes. Meanwhile Claire is not only Whacker's 'mum' but also a fantastic social media manager. I really am incredibly lucky – as are the dogs – to have such a talented bunch of people supporting the cause. Not to mention the entire army of online followers and all the amazing people who make kind donations.

Managing to finally secure charity status means that all the money we raise will be stretched that little bit further thanks to receiving tax exemptions and benefits. Any boost to our ability to fundraise is of course very welcome and makes a difference. We've also found some great trustees and other crucial people to help make this all work seamlessly and transparently.

I want Happy Doggo to be a global organisation as the problem of street dogs is a global one and as an official charity, with a certificate and a smart new stamp (which I really do like using) we can dream even bigger.

If you ask me where I want to be in ten years' time, I'll say that I want to be doing exactly what I'm doing today, but just on a wider scale to help even more dogs avoid a life of suffering. I'll stay in Thailand where I'm happy and finally at peace with myself, but I want to recruit brilliant people here as well as in other parts of the world too, so it's less about me personally and the focus is all on Happy Doggo the organisation driving all the work.

Seeing the official red and white logo for Happy Doggo for the first time popping up everywhere felt great, and like the crazy, ambitious plans that had buzzed around in my head for so long these were all becoming real things. I imagine I felt like something parents feel on the day they realise their little babies have got all grown-up and turned into responsible adults. You're incredibly proud and yet also slightly dazed that you ever got there.

I can push myself so hard and get cross with myself if things don't happen immediately. Like once I'd decided on building Tina's Hospital, I wanted it up and running now … as in right now.

But getting Happy Doggo turned into an official and well-functioning organisation, of which the hospital would be a crucial part, I knew was a real achievement. It made me realise how far I'd come in just a few short years, from being a guy wearing flip-flops on a moped feeding kibble to some jungle strays to someone at the helm of a proper organisation which was helping thousands of dogs. I'd co-founded business ventures in the past, but becoming the actual CEO of Happy Doggo was very special. And I still get to wear flip-flops.

I had a website created to give everyone an overview of what we are trying to do, and right on the homepage where you first land there's a dynamic tally for people to see the three key statistics rising in real time. These are: how many dogs we feed each day (over 1,000), how many dogs in total we have had sterilised (approaching 70,000), as well as how many dogs we've re-homed with new families (60-odd and counting.) Of course by the time you read this, these numbers will change. In fact if you can stop reading now, open up the internet and please check for me. What are the numbers? I'll always smile knowing that each reader will potentially see a different number. I hope!

I also wanted to include some of the dogs' stories – and Tina's photo is right there at the top. I know I post a lot about what we do on social media, and I try to make it fun and (hopefully) uplifting, but the website would complement this I thought, and offer all the important information I don't post on social media. It points people in the right direction if they want to help or donate or adopt dogs, as well as answering some of the more common questions they might have.

For instance, we're often asked whether people can come and visit the land or volunteer here, and sadly the answer is no. We don't have a scheme running but this is something I'd like to happen eventually if the number of requests we get daily are anything to go by. It's a popular request, believe me. We're still a small team caring for multiple sick dogs so the capacity is limited; there's only about 16 dogs staying at the sanctuary at any one time.

While we don't have a volunteer programme right now, if anyone is planning to visit Thailand and or Koh Samui, and would like to help us get a dog to their forever home, we're always looking for flight volunteers. Essentially this is a human offering to chaperone the dogs and make sure they safely get to their destination.

There's also stuff on there for anyone interested in adopting, there's pictures and life stories about the ones who need re-homing. Adoptions are wonderful, and that's the dream for the dogs who don't fare well on the streets or who really need their own human to thrive.

People fall in love with certain dogs all the time, me included, and ask if they can adopt them. But not every dog is suitable for adoptions; some have health issues that wouldn't make it fair on the dogs or the new owners, and it also depends on how likely they are to adapt well to a different home, with potentially other pets or children. And quite frequently they're not put up for adoption because there is no urgent need – many dogs are perfectly happy and well cared for on the street where we can feed them and still treat them for parasites, sterilise them and give any preventative or necessary medicines and vaccines. Many healthy, strong dogs would prefer to live this way. Re-homing a dog takes months – it's a long, drawn-out process that takes up space at the sanctuary needed for dogs who are really sick. If the street dogs are happy and healthy, we can actually help more dogs by leaving them where they are.

Happy Doggo Land was never going to be a place just to home dogs – it's a stepping stone or a pit stop, a safe place to recover until they're well enough to survive on the streets. Sometimes I have to explain that to people who simply want me to take them all in. And sometimes I have to remind myself why I can't.

Shaq, in fact, was a dog that I thought very, very closely about adopting and taking into my house. I don't often do this, because I don't want to collect dogs for myself. But things with Shaq had been so traumatic, and I'd become so close to him, that I genuinely longed to take him in.

The six weeks I spent with him made me love him so dearly that sometimes it's very hard for me to see him and think of him as a street dog and not my own. Although I have to move on and think of all the many, many other dogs that need help, Shaq will always have a special place in my heart. He's the best and bravest boy there ever was, showing incredible resilience and a will to live that inspires everyone who meets him.

One night I found myself thinking about finding Shaq a forever home. I was so happy to see the end of his suffering that placing him with people who would care for him felt like the right thing to do.

By then, watching how well he was doing since the tumour had gone, I realised in my heart that Shaq is 100 per cent unadulterated pure street dog. It wouldn't suit his style or character to be confined by four walls and given an owner – however loving they might be.

Many of the dogs we help have lived on the streets for years. They're independent and they like their freedom; some might not like human contact or feeling cooped up and so these dogs would never be put up for re-homing. It just wouldn't be suitable.

Not only that, but we knew of a nice place for Shaq to dwell 'in the wild'; there were two friends of his there, and they lived beside a house which was a safe place. What's more, the people there were able, and up for, giving him the necessary food and medicines.

So that's where I released him. I go and visit him there once every couple of weeks and bring him sausages. He's as healthy and happy as can be and it was the right decision.

But all the dogs are unique, and you have to consider them as individuals when thinking about what kind of place will suit them best.

Cindy Crawford, for instance, we could never have put back on the street like Shaq. Ultimately, we knew it was best for Cindy to be moved from the land where there were always going to be too many treats and the potential to pile the weight back on. It was clear that she would be better off with one responsible and loving owner who could carefully monitor her weight and diet.

We had initially been thinking about adopting her overseas, and there were hundreds of inquiries because Cindy was that popular. But in the end Lana Chapman, some readers may already know, had been taking Cindy out on many of her walks, came forward. She had been thinking about adopting Cindy for a while but was shy about bringing this up with me she admitted, because she knew I had been looking at applications and didn't want to deprive some other loving owner of adopting Little Cindy (or perhaps not so little – she's got a stubborn final kilo still to go). When I heard she was keen, I was delighted, it seemed absolutely perfect. It made complete sense that Cindy would be better off not travelling abroad if she could stay locally instead.

So Cindy ended up finding her forever home living with Lana and her partner, Danni, and their other two dogs – and I promise you that loveable bubbly lady has a *wonderful* life. The kind of dogs who make good pets are the ones who love humans (as Tina did) and they enjoy a comfortable life, and they're not too bothered about running free. Dogs we help who are like this are great candidates for adoption.

It might seem random if you follow us online about how we choose which dogs get adopted. But I promise you, a lot of consideration goes into making these decisions. We think about how they came to the land in the first place, whether the dog had been targeted before – like Hope or King Whacker had been – because street dogs tend to migrate back to the same territory they've always lived in, as they're creatures of habit. Even if we put them back on the streets elsewhere, they'll tend to find their way back to the old spot. So if they've been targeted in the past, either by humans or other dogs, that can be dangerous. As they can't stay on the land forever taking up space for those who really need it, they become prime candidates for finding a home.

Another thing we consider is whether they can live in a pack. For whatever reason (and it's not usually clear to humans) some dogs just aren't accepted into a gang. Even if they get on well with other dogs, some will live by themselves and have a lonely life, or other dogs can regularly be picked on and end up with injuries and feeling miserable. As they'll always go back to the same spot, it's not safe for them out there.

We've now devised the following five-step adoption process which takes about four to six months – so it's quite lengthy – but means each dog has the best chance of getting settled into a new life:

Rehabilitation and behavioural assessment

When a dog arrives at Happy Doggo Land, they've often been traumatised, or have illnesses or hidden injuries. Things like tick fever, heartworm, parasitic diseases and little wounds are standard, and it's not fair on the dog or the new owners to adopt them until they're healthy and well. And we couldn't fly them if they weren't. So we work hard at restoring their health, getting them nourished with the best foods and rehabilitation under the guidance of vets. It's not just about their physical healing; this is the time when they really need love, comfort and trust-building. We have to look at each dog's behaviour, and start preparing them so they're ready for any new family.

Applications and interviews

Our main aim for the dogs we re-home is to find them the perfect place where they'll be happy. That also includes getting the right dog for the people applying. After all, a super-active dog isn't going to be ideal for a sedentary family, and vice versa. A nervous dog wouldn't be great for people with small, loud kids, and a dog who requires a lot of attention won't work for people who are out all day.

We try to match the right dogs with the right people through a thorough application form and a minimum of two in-depth interviews. Applicants are asked about the people they live with, other pets, their daily routine and told as much about the dog as possible.

While we give them as much information as we can, we can't replicate a home and family situation at the land so we make sure all applicants are really committed to the reality of owning a street dog and know the potential challenges.

Medical preparation

Often, it can be months between us picking a home for each pup and them actually travelling. This is because the dogs are effectively 'quarantined' at the land while we complete the required tests for them to meet the import requirements of their new home country. This usually takes between two and three months and during this time we organise their flights and a flight volunteer who will accompany them to their forever home.

Travel and logistics

Flying can be a pretty big ordeal for dogs. Most have never left their little patch of territory and the land so it's a huge overload of smells, sights and sounds for them to travel through an airport.

Before they fly, we try our best to get them used to their crates. Street dogs are used to being free and can often feel scared of being put in a crate. We'll feed them their dinners in the crates and encourage them to see them as a nice place to be. We'll also get them used to drinking water from the bottles in the crate so they don't go many hours without any hydration.

Then we get them to Bangkok airport via pet taxi where they usually meet up with their flight volunteer, who makes sure the dogs are safely on the plane and picks them up at the other side.

Settling into their new home

When dogs arrive at their new home, some will be happy and excited. However, it's usually been a big journey for them and they can be really overwhelmed. Rather than plan a big welcome party, we recommend new owners use the first few hours and days to let their new family member decompress and get used to their surroundings. Not all dogs conform to this exactly, but we always recommend that new owners follow the 3/3/3 rule when bringing home a new dog.

After three months have passed and everything has gone well, we consider an adoption to be complete. While there will almost certainly still be work ahead, at this point your dog will truly be a part of your home.

Another thing that we have to consider when adopting is not all dogs are able to even fly. Some dogs, like snub-nosed ones (formally referred to as 'brachycephalic' breeds), aren't allowed on aeroplanes in case they have breathing problems, which are more common in breeds like bulldogs, pugs and boxers because of their anatomy. The worry is that with the air-pressurised cabins, they could struggle with their breathing, so they cannot be re-homed outside of Thailand (unless they were shipped, I suppose, though that wouldn't be fair for long periods).

Bully breeds of dogs are also banned from flying. I'm sure we've all read plenty about these muscular and stocky dogs in the news. They can be quite strong and have a reputation for being aggressive though it really depends on whether they've been properly socialised and trained. Hank, my most recent dog housemate, is a bulldog, he's affectionate, goofy and a bit stubborn – he hates the rain so I literally have to drag him on a lead for walks some days in the monsoon season. So a dog like Hank wouldn't be able to fly (not that he'd want to thank you very much).

Different countries have different rules concerning dog adoptions, so elsewhere in Thailand, the USA, the UK, countries in the EU and Singapore is fine, but not Australia or Canada where there are more restrictive quarantine rules. I love looking at the map of the world sometimes and seeing that our very own Happy Doggos are now dotted across the globe with their new families, hand-picked especially for them – and loving their lives in their new homes.

And the really lovely thing is that once the dogs are adopted they all still remain part of the wider Happy Doggo family and we keep in touch with each other's news. The new 'mums' of the dogs – the wonderful ladies who adopted Rodney, King Whacker and McMuffin – have all gone on to become actual mums with their own *human* babies since they adopted the dogs. So the family is ever growing. I might have to start a little family tree if this trend continues …

CHAPTER SEVENTEEN

'TWAS THE NIGHT BEFORE CHRISTMAS ...

Planning Tina's Hospital remained at the forefront of my mind throughout every coming and going at the land. By that November, I was just so impatient to get it happening, and because I'd told everyone in such a fanfare about the great plan everyone was naturally asking about it ten to fifteen times a day. Everybody was so super-supportive and just wanted to see it built.

I honestly wished I could start digging the foundations myself there and then, right beside Tina and Snoop's resting place, but I'd at least managed to get an agreement to expand the land that I currently rented on a long lease for the sanctuary. This would allow the hospital to be physically built on that spot next to the sanctuary down Hope Avenue which was clearly the most practical place as well as being an important and somewhat emotional decision for me. The whole point of Tina's Hospital was that it was created in her name and I wanted her incredible spirit to infuse the whole place. I'd kept the little felt Tina I'd been given beside my bed (she was later joined by a little felt

Snoop). Seeing both the dogs' handmade figures gave me that extra boost of energy every day.

It was all taking shape, but there was just loads of fiddly stuff that needed to be done that most of us wouldn't know about, unless you were a builder yourself. I'd need to run the hospital as a non-profit organisation (and for that I'd need to set up a Thai foundation), permits for operating with vets and other staff personnel things to consider. I needed to hammer out the full budget for the build, and then present it along with how I planned to secure ongoing funding. One thing that became abundantly clear was that a lot of funding was needed.

So many people had been asking how they could help. Along with all the proceeds from the first book we created three lovely products all to be sold for the hospital cause in time for Christmas. There were Tina t-shirts (I wear mine pretty much constantly and with a lot of pride), a wall calendar with everyone's favourite dogs pictured (lovely Cindy Crawford was Miss January) and a gorgeous colouring book for children. I receive so many cards, letters and drawings from kids all over the world so I wanted to give something back to say thank you for all the beautiful cards that mean so much to me.

I'd accepted that my initial hopes to open it three months after her death, then six months when that didn't work out, were both too optimistic. In the end, a year also seemed unrealistic for a plan this ambitious. I decided to extend the official deadline. I sincerely hope we'd have it finished on 18 August 2025, to mark the two-year anniversary of Tina's passing. And we'd open it at 4.45 p.m., the exact time she died.

I often found myself wondering about those hours I spent with her in the hammock. Not in a maudlin kind of way though, but more in trying to channel that real sense of peace and rare clarity about the meaning of life that I'd found in those final moments with her.

With Christmas fast approaching I was also worried about old Jumbo. They say things come in threes and I had this uneasy premonition that it could be him. I sensed with sadness that Jumbo was slowing down, he had late-stage kidney failure and his health was declining every day.

He was the one who'd so loved sausages, so I promised to keep bringing him his sausages and not let him suffer when the time came.

I've now spent several Christmases in Thailand, and I'm used to the fact that there's no snow and I'll still be wearing my trusty shorts and flip-flops as I tuck into traditional turkey dinners. You even get to see the odd Father Christmas strolling around, albeit with elephants and not reindeer. It can feel slightly surreal.

But I like the fact that celebrating the big day out here is so different from how it was growing up. And my memories and associations with the day aren't all particularly happy ones anyway.

Christmas is a hard time for everyone. It's a time for family but what if you don't have a family or your family situation is a difficult one? It can be the most isolating and lonely time.

Christmas time always reminds me of my self-destructive past. For me this season was always the toughest one to get through, and those festive days were much harder than the 'normal' days, although when it comes to alcoholism hardly any day is a normal day.

Fast forward and on Christmas Eve 2023, I had the great pleasure of taking Sybille for a nice lunch to thank her for all she'd done for me and the dogs that year. She's one of the people I rely on the most, and because she's a trained doctor I'm always asking her medical sort of questions, too. She might not be quite as knowledgeable as an actual vet, but she's got more understanding of that side of things than me.

Sybille was explaining to me, as we tucked into a traditional turkey dinner with a Thai-style twist, that Christmas is one of the busiest times of year for emergencies. The emergency departments are rammed with people having domestic accidents, like setting fire to Christmas puddings, or pulling crackers too near eyes, or kids getting Lego rammed up their nose. It's also when older people can get seriously sick with winter bugs, or partygoers have a little too much to drink and get hurt while being clumsy.

In a similar way we reckoned it was also a period when the street dogs could be a bit more vulnerable too. Tourists flocked to the island to escape colder Christmases back at home, and naturally they're all drinking and partying which is fun for them but can mean carnage for the local dogs. Dogs can walk on broken glass or eat party poppers or get knocked over by more traffic.

So there's always plenty of frantic rushing around after the animals trying to patch them up as well as just some decent dinners into their empty bellies. Just earlier that morning I'd been busy helping one poor creature who'd been a casualty of a hit and run and needed a broken leg fixing up. I can't wait for the hospital to be up and running as it would be the perfect place to take animals facing these kinds of emergencies.

And lo and behold, just as we were chatting, my phone showed I had a new WhatsApp notification. A dog had been burnt and, while the initial photos didn't look *too* bad, I knew there was more work for the day needed. We skipped the pudding and headed straight down to the 7-Eleven where the dog had found refuge.

Immediately I realised things were worse for this little girl than how they'd seemed in the picture and we were just in time to help.

The poor mite was cowering inside the shop as the staff had let her inside to keep her cooler in the air-conditioning. She was a female bitch, mostly white with a sweet little brown face and terrified dark eyes. It seemed she had been splashed with hot oil and water, resulting in severe burns. Ouch. Clearly she was in agony, and when we approached her to pick her up her natural instinct was to snap and she tried to bite my arm off. It wasn't an aggressive bite though, it was really just a protective 'I'm in pain here, stay away from me!' kind of yelp. She didn't know me, she obviously didn't trust me, and she was trembling with fear and hurt.

Her whole leg was burnt. The skin was tender and raw, and I winced at the sight of it. Burns really are horribly painful, and it must have been unbearable for her. How the hell had she ever got this? And why had no-one then bothered to take proper care of her? I felt myself fuming inside that here she was on her own. I gathered that there had been some talk among the locals about getting her to the vets and trying to treat the little thing with medical care, but nobody had any money. They just hadn't known what to do with her and no-one was taking responsibility.

Once Sybille and I had managed to transport her as carefully as possible, driving super-slowly in the car and avoiding as many bumps along the way as possible, the vet gave her a once-over. The agony she was in as the vet had cleaned her wounds was heartbreaking to witness and, other than giving her painkillers, plus some other medicines that calmed her down and sort of regulated her temperature, there wasn't a lot to be done. She was in a bad, bad way alright. And when the vet needed a name for her for the records, I quickly said 'Eve' – it was Christmas Eve after all.

After that check-up, as gently as possible again, we transported our new friend to the safety of the land and made her as comfortable as we could with the softest blankets in her own little suite. But Eve was still shaking and struggling to control her temperature and had no interest in food or drink or taking herself off to the toilet.

I worried about her overnight, and wondered if Eve would wake up on Christmas morning alive or dead. I woke up on Christmas Day to a small miracle: she was still with us in the morning, though she was understandably shaky and a little wary. After she'd tried to bite me that first time I was also nervous about how I should approach her. I rang Sybille to tell her the good news that Eve was hanging in there.

But Sybille explained that the recovery from these kinds of injuries and accidents can be complicated. She had looked after human victims of burns in the past and warned that the biggest issue can be that when the damaged skin naturally forms a protective layer on top of the burn, what happens is that it traps all the bacteria under it, which means patients – whether dog or human – can very quickly get into trouble with infections.

This is more likely to occur when the burn hasn't been treated properly which can cause an infection to fester under the hard, caked skin. Not for the first time, I was grateful to have Sybille's knowledge and experience, but I did seriously start to fret about little Eve's future.

In the coming days I feared Eve's little body might have given up several times, but as she relaxed in my company, and the wounds started to appear as if they might be healing, it became clear that underneath Eve had a lovely nature. I wish dogs could talk – I wanted to know what had happened to her. What we'd been told was that oil and water had spilled onto her as she had somehow got too close to someone cooking. I couldn't really envisage how this would have happened in reality and we never got to the real truth of the story.

We have probably all had some kind of minor burn at some stage – a little mishap in the kitchen on the hob, or picking up a hot pan without oven gloves. I must have done that hundreds of times myself back in my cheffing days, and I know full well that burning sensation is agony even if in just the tiniest of spots. You think it's fine and then you get in the shower or something and the pain re-starts again. Not fun. So I could tell how much it must have hurt Eve to have this sensation covering her entire, scalded leg. Sybille did a brilliant job of tending to the wound, keeping it cleaned as well as letting it air.

Eve's lack of appetite was a worry though. I had bought a leg of lamb that my friend and I were going to cook, well my friend was going to do most, all of the cooking. As the smell filled the room I noticed little Eve showing some interest in the food. It must have smelt pretty good, if I say so myself, and her little nose started sniffing and twitching.

I pulled off some of the tender meat and passed it to her mouth where she happily took it in and looked at me with big eyes that I could swear looked a little brighter.

That was the first sign that she was maybe going to be OK.

She'd developed a funny crab-like walk, the leg was clearly painful to rest her weight on or bend so she'd taken to walking sideways. It took several weeks to get her walking properly, and there would be little setbacks where she would bump her leg and the whole skin would flare up angrily again.

What was nice to see was the budding friendship between Eve and Cindy Crawford. I used to keep them both in the office a lot of the time. For Eve it was better for her not to be in with the rough and tumble of the other dogs, while Cindy Crawford mainly needed to be kept away from eating other dogs' dinners! So the pair of them hung out together in the office a lot and became best of friends.

Once she was able to walk and even run like a healthy dog, Eve really came out of her shell and once she'd decided that she liked me she started following me everywhere. She even became a little possessive of me and would sometimes snap if I paid attention to the other dogs. I felt it was a sign that here was an incredibly loving and loyal dog who would really thrive if given her own human to take care of her.

So the final piece of Eve's puzzle was finding her a forever home – and the wonderful news came that a loving family in England wanted to adopt her. They'd been so taken with her story and resilient spirit that they decided to come out and visit here in Thailand, making Eve's transition to her new life easier.

Her fur will never grow back fully – she will always carry the scars of being a burn victim – but she's pain-free and now living her best life in England with her new family. I gather her and the cat sometimes have a few 'heated discussions' about which of them is boss, but she's settled in nicely and is very well looked after and loved.

Seeing Eve off at the airport, adorned with a little pink bow and greeting her new family with joy, was a moment of pure magic. This is what all our efforts are about – giving these animals the second chance they deserve.

CHAPTER EIGHTEEN

WELCOME TO THE LAND OF DOGS

At any given time we are taking care of 16 dogs. It's not generally very glamorous I'm afraid, so I tend not to share much of the basics on social media.

So the days start early for us, and the mornings are the busiest times. Generally by 6 a.m. we're letting the dogs out of their little suites so they can go to the toilet, stretch their legs and eat some breakfast. We cook all of our dog food in the central kitchen; sometimes it smells so good I'm tempted to taste it. That's what I've always wanted – for it to be nutritious but also as good as anything I'd want to eat. We make sure their diet is fresh, nutritious and as cost effective as can be, so for example we'll add carrots and use the gravy to hold it all together. It's my favourite part of the day, picking up the food parcels that our chef has prepared ready to load on my moped. I'm kind of like a doggie Santa. We feed them quite far apart, people have noticed, but that's only to make sure the weaker and younger ones don't miss out. And to make sure they don't turn on each other.

In the mornings the dogs are generally pretty hyper and need to eat and run off steam; the younger ones especially have the high energy of teenagers and we put them into their little packs of friends. One of the biggest jobs we do, which takes up a massive amount of time, is taking them on walks. Luckily, I have a series of friends who come and help on a daily basis to walk the dogs. They get a great workout and most days I'm clocking up well over the recommended step count too, usually about 15,000 to 20,000 steps.

Some of the dogs are taken on leads but not all; it really just depends on their personality and whether they're going to bolt off or have a go at other dogs or humans, which we need to avoid.

There's lots of the nitty-gritty stuff that goes on behind the scenes, and that's what actually takes up the most time. As we're in the middle of the jungle there's no natural water source, which meant that we had to drill a deep well that went down 150 feet to get to the water, which then fills up the tanks. And to fill up they need electricity, so we have installed solar panels on top of our roof.

Being off grid takes some planning, because we need fridges to keep food fresh and all the medicines at a low temperature to make sure they don't spoil and work how they're supposed to do.

We've constantly washing blankets and towels and the like, as dogs are like babies in that they create a fair amount of laundry. And we're lucky enough to have our handyman because there's always a water leak or little things here and there that need fixing, like the fans we use to keep the animals cool on the days when the sun is really scorching.

The weather is probably one of the most treacherous things, so shade and plenty of water are a priority, and proper shelters from the monsoons, but there's other random dangers that might sound absolutely mad to you at home right now, when your heating might be switched on and you're sitting down after a long day at work.

Out here there's things like snakes to worry about (and don't get me wrong, I'm not saying these worries are any worse – just different). So we have the little green grass ones that are common and they're not too bad, but we've also had big cobras. Cobras have potent venom which can cause serious harm like being paralysed or breathing issues or even death if they bite you and you're not treated in time. The dogs don't want that and neither do I or any of the lovely volunteers. So we have to keep an eye out and call in locals who are experts at dealing with those dangers.

And did you know how dangerous coconut trees can be? When the coconuts get to a certain weight and fall off their branches there's every chance they'll whack into the head of any dog (or human) who is lying under it for much-needed shade. That could do serious damage we don't need. And we also have to dispose of our rubbish: it's not like back at home where you put your different wheelie bins out and they're collected by the nice bin men each week. There's not those facilities here, so everything needs to get taken off the land and sorted out and put in the appropriate place. Running the whole set-up as sustainably as possible is really important to us here. We live in a beautiful place and want to look after it.

There's a lot of driving around usually on any one day to various vets for treatment or checks, and I know that this aspect of the work would be easier when we have a hospital on site.

All in all, a day at the sanctuary does take it out of you, and I often like to sit quietly and recharge in a hammock with a dog who needs a bit of special attention. Even if it's for just ten minutes. But we've also learned that when the dogs are well exercised, stimulated with some play time, and have bellies full with food, they generally sleep for the rest of the day. And that makes for a happy sanctuary.

Everything is set up to welcome sick dogs and dogs who need our help, and with Tina's Hospital it will be the place where we can fix them up, too. It's growing and expanding with each day and I am so, so proud of what we have built. This truly feels like my family. But there is nothing like reconnecting with your family, so I was over the moon when my dad, Ronan, came to stay with me. It was the first time he'd come to Thailand as well as it being the first time I'd seen him in three and a half or maybe even four years. I think we were both nervous and excited about this. It was so lovely to reunite and reconnect with him in person after all that time, and introduce Dad to all the dogs he'd only seen on a screen previously and show him how my life looks and works out here.

When I was in the depths of my addiction, of course my dad – and my mum, Kathleen – despite their differences and past history were desperately worried about me. Any parent must go through hell having to watch helplessly while their child goes down a chaotic path to self-destruction. I dare say I've given both of them a few more grey hairs from worry and stress over the years. And I hope they both know how very sorry I am now for all the pain and hurt that caused them.

Our family generally keeps in touch via group WhatsApps, along with the odd video call and phone conversations too. I imagine many of you have similar set-ups with relatives as well as friends. And you'll probably have all noticed that WhatsApp is great for swapping in-jokes and little personal comments, and birthday wishes and the like. It's a nice and easy way of keeping in touch and showing we're thinking of each other despite being separated physically by such a great distance. But on the flipside, it's all too easy with those groups to feel like you don't *really* know what's going on in someone's life. Most of the exchanges we have are so casual that you feel like you know everything in some way, but also none of the deeper stuff that's happening and how they're really feeling about all the little things and bigger things going on in their lives.

My dad follows our journey with the dogs on social media too, so he knows as much as anyone else about the progress we're making out here. Absolutely he does. But it was special for him to be here in the flesh and really understand it all. I even cooked a dinner for him: we had a little barbeque on the beach. I have to confess, that was probably the first time I'd cooked (if assembling a barbeque counts as 'cooking') in many, many months. And come to think of it, that might in fact have been the last meal I've prepared myself in many months! It's not that I've lost my passion for food since the days of being a chef, it's more that my passion for doing good work is simply more my priority these days. But cooking (or not cooking) is something that I get asked about a lot for some reason.

We didn't have *loads* of deep chats about life, I have to admit. I guess that only happens in films. I had to keep going. I couldn't shirk my duties, not for anyone.

Then one night we did sit down just by the hammock. I was telling him about my life and how happy I was that I had found my purpose in this corner of the world that's not mine. As I began to speak about the last few years, I felt something heavy pull me into the ground. I felt acceptance and the roots that I laid in Thailand, on Hope Avenue, with these wonderful volunteers, these unlikely hero dogs, where I realised I was home. I'd been searching for something and that something found me here. Right under the stars, in that moment as I was filling in my dad on the ordinary everyday life I lead here. Then, as if completely naturally, we got on to talking about the grief of losing Tina and Snoop in such a short span of time. He listened to every word, as if those words were filling in lost time for both of us, and at the end he offered a simple, 'I'm proud of you, son, just like Tina and Snoop are. You'll be OK.' I didn't reply, I didn't need to – everything was just right and the moment was crowned in silence.

That meant a lot to me. I never take my sobriety for granted. I know it's something I have to decide each and every day – do not go back to drinking. Even when times are tough. My life is so much better without alcohol in it. It felt important to show Dad this, the older and tiny bit wiser version of me.

Dad is retired now and living in Belgium, but he was in his element with the novelty of being here in the tropical heat, eating tasty new foods and being surrounded by my world.

Once my dad had left I was able to regroup and focus on the building plans. I had a hospital to build! I couldn't believe my luck when some wonderful architects had offered to draw up some plans for Tina's Hospital. That golden retriever had touched the hearts of so many people around the world in all sorts of unexpected ways.

One such person was Danny Forster, a New York based architect and expert on design. I hadn't heard of him before, but he'd been on TV shows in the States and people in America might know him from appearances on programmes like Discovery Channel's *Build It Bigger*, where he explored large construction projects around the world. He was also executive producer for something called *Rising: Rebuilding Ground Zero*, a documentary film that Steven Spielberg (yes *the* Hollywood director) was involved in. *Rising* followed the reconstruction of the World Trade Center site after the September 11 attacks in 2001, and as you'd imagine was all about resilience, hope and the rebuilding of a community.

Honestly, it was just gobsmacking that somehow this bigwig guy had heard of our mission and was keen to support it. But Danny is mad about dogs, so had reached out personally online and offered for Danny Foster & Architecture, his world-renowned firm, to design the hospital *free of charge*. I hastily googled the work they did and couldn't really believe our luck this was happening. He'd worked on some of the most prestigious projects you can imagine, for clients with literally billions of dollars and grand plans. And here I was speaking to him on the phone, and then over Zoom, and hearing his passion for Tina and our dogs.

One of the first times I met him on a video he was dialling in from hospital where his partner had just had a baby … that day! I said, 'You're mad! Get off this call and be with her!' But even on a massively important day like the birth of his first child, Danny was still thinking and planning for

Tina's Hospital. Insane, I know. But absolutely brilliant that he was so committed to this. I will be eternally grateful.

I realised what had all begun as a shouted, angry promise I made into thin air after Tina had taken her last breath had become a bigger dream than I could ever have hoped for. It seemed like this nondescript patch of abandoned jungle would one day soon be home to a world-class facility for treating sick dogs. The very kind of dog Tina had once been herself.

Danny was really keen to start work on the 'conceptual design phase' of the project. Which basically means what it would look like and how it all would all work in day-to-day practice. And Danny and his team put so much work into it and so much care and consideration. The regular meetings we had to discuss it all were called 'workshops' where we were asked about all sorts of things like our feelings, not just the practical elements of putting a building together. He wanted to create a special place that *felt* harmonious too, once you were inside it. He wanted to ensure that the architectural design reflected Tina's spirit and also expressed our story.

Architecture isn't my area of expertise, so to be honest I would have thought a hospital is just, well … a case of putting up a building and putting some X-ray rooms and consulting rooms in there, that sort of thing. But over the course of several months of chatting to DF&A, having meetings every week, they came up with a concept which

I just adored so much. It was like they totally got the feeling in my heart that I would never have been able to translate to an actual 3D building design in a million years.

Of course we needed to be practical and lay out all the plans, but it became about so much more than just the building. They really understood what was needed for the animals we'd take in and care for, and about the spirit in which it had all been inspired. They understood about Tina, and they wanted to make something that would last.

The architects came up with the brilliant idea of making Tina's grave (where I'd always imagined the hospital would be built) an actual focus in itself. They talked about turning that very area around her burial place into a kind of walkway through the hospital.

I'd always wanted her spirit to infuse the whole place, but I'd never imagined it would ever be possible to give it an actual *physical* focus. I'd just had no idea it was even possible.

It all made me buzz with excitement. This idea that the building would literally wrap around the grave in the middle so that anybody who came to visit, or any of us ourselves who worked at the sanctuary, could come out and have a reflective moment by Tina's resting place felt so special. It would truly be a space where Tina's spirit and passion for life could continue to inspire us every day. All the thought behind the building's design and layout was just outstanding, a tribute fitting for the truly remarkable impact this one dog had made on our lives.

Of course, the architectural team had also listened so thoughtfully to all the things I'd explained would be needed – like plenty of space for the dogs that need to be cared for overnight to stay in, the emergency wards, the X-ray rooms, the consulting rooms. And once we had finalised the designs we agreed that I would travel to New York to meet Danny and his amazing team in person to review the final design. I couldn't wait, I was that excited.

Visiting their office was a very surreal experience. As I walked into the fancy offices I had no idea what to expect. I could tell from their faces and the presentation they had prepared, and which was placed on the conference table, that they had put a lot of work into this. All in Tina's name. They had this wonderful, kind but expectant look on their faces as they pushed the button to show me the first slide. My heart exploded as I sat through 20 minutes of mind-blowing slides about what they had planned. I was utterly speechless. A whole building sculpted around Tina and her resting place. The sun was piercing through the windows as I drifted off in my reverie. As everybody talked about plumbing and slopes, I thought about Tina and thought, 'Bloody hell! Can you believe this, old girl?'

And then it would be a case of needing to pair up DF&A with a local Thailand-based architect to help manage construction on the ground. In the empty space that had just been abandoned jungle, we would soon be doing great work to save and improve lives.

There were still a lot of details that needed to be teased out, and people were asking all sorts of valid questions. But the one question that always makes me chuckle is people asking 'Are you actually going to call it "Tina's Hospital for Dogs Who Aren't Doing So Good?"' – and the answer to that is yes, absolutely!

The amount of things I had to remember to do and the decisions I still had to make were keeping me up at night. Need to raise more money, permits, licences, building regulations, all that stuff. And we'd need to build a concrete road into the land to replace the dirt track that was being used, proper access would be required and that all had to be officially signed off.

I can't lie, it was daunting knowing what needed to be raised in terms of cash. There were some nights not sleeping too well. And more days feeling anxious than I'd like to admit to at this point.

We were building a hospital from scratch! So here's where we are at the time of going to print:

Road building

We've just finished building a 120-yard concrete road into the hospital so as the trucks, diggers, workers and ultimately the dogs and humans can get into the jungle. We've had to foot the cost of the build ourselves but seeing that road there is a concrete sign that things are happening and the hospital is being built.

Added new utilities

We've worked with the local council to run new power and utility lines into the land ready for the build. This seems pretty trivial but we are in the middle of the jungle so getting the electricity we need, the water pressure and even Wifi there for a hospital has been a huge challenge. However, we've dug up Hope Avenue and have all the utilities we need.

Field hospital

With everything taking so long and with such an urgent need to actually start treating sick dogs we have what we call a field hospital up and running. This is made up of three shipping containers that are stacked with all the equipment for the main hospital and the staff to run it. The field hospital is effectively a big clinic and it allows the professional vet staff to treat dogs in the same way they would in the big hospital but in a more confined space. As soon as the big hospital is finished the field hospital will be dismantled.

Architect planning

Our New York architects are working with our Thai team and we have the building completely costed with detailed drawings and every small detail planned out. They are working across time zones and have a design that matches the local terrain as well as being beautiful and highly functional as a hospital. From the moment we started that process it took a full year.

Foundation digging

As you read this the hospital build has started and is due to open in late 2025. I wish things could move faster but it isn't for a lack of hard work, funding or will on our part, Permits, plans and building a hospital take a lot longer than I would have ever imagined.

I find myself stopping by Tina's grave nearly every day. I wait until nobody else is around, then I just sit there and talk to her. I tell her about the fancy New York architects, the people climbing mountains in her name and her t-shirts with her face that were being worn all over the world now. Tina would have been too modest to ever think it was all down to her. She'd have been more worried about how everyone else was feeling, and if she could give out some more love and attention.

But this dream of Tina's Hospital was all down to her, and now it really was all about to start becoming a reality. I could almost visualise walking into a reception packed full of beautiful Tina memorabilia and know she would be grinning about all of this in whatever canine heaven she was in. I imagined her up there somewhere, wearing her favourite bandana, with a tennis ball at her feet, and my lovely Snoop next to her for company. I couldn't help smiling.

CHAPTER NINETEEN

WHEN BILLY BURST INTO TOWN

I'd been out in the teeming Thai rain feeding the dogs, and had just sat down with a coffee and a lovely pain au chocolat fresh from the oven and was idly scrolling through the news on my phone when the familiar ping went off. 'This dog has been slashed,' it read, the message from a guy I knew who worked in a nearby school. And I braced myself for the picture that came next. *Jesus.*

I truly couldn't believe the photo on my screen. I know I say this a lot but things can still shock and appal me. What I saw was barely even recognisable as a dog. There was a mass of grey-black fur filling most of the frame. What I thought were his haunches had that browny colour that comes through in a tattered and uncared for coat. In the foreground were two recognisable doggy ears … and then an ugly red and purple slash wound.

I put down the coffee cup in one hand. And I had to look away from the phone held in the other and drew a breath. I closed my eyes for a few seconds. I felt a wave of exhaustion suddenly.

TINA

Aside from feeding the dogs in the rain that morning, I had been working really hard and was feeling a low level yet constant stress about all that needed to be done for the hospital. I'd struggled to get out of bed and feel motivated that morning and had even wondered whether I might have been able to take a modest break, perhaps even a little kip after my breakfast. But … it wasn't to be after looking at that picture.

For as soon as I saw that small, vulnerable face I just knew. *I have to go and get this little guy.* Any kind of abuse to this day makes me feel sick and shaky from the bottom of my soul. It takes me right back to when I was younger. I'm immediately transported to those dark, lonely moments sitting on top of the stairs hearing the shouts, the crashes and the crying that my mum was going through. Knowing she was being hurt and feeling so completely powerless as a skinny kid who was ill-equipped to deal with adult problems and just being terrified for my mum. I don't think that painful memory ever leaves you really, once it's in your head and heart. And now, whenever someone, or some creature, has been subjected to any kind of mistreatment, it takes me right back to feeling useless and agonised exactly like I did as a kid.

I couldn't finish the pastry. I got in the car and drove down straightaway to find the poor thing. The guy who had sent the message was someone I knew a little bit: he worked in a nearby school, and we'd recently been taking kids to the sanctuary and educating them about the work and the dogs. So he was on our side and wanted to help. He had coaxed this little dog into the dry of the school, and had kept him there overnight. When we arrived there we could see immediately what a sorry state the poor mutt was in.

He was a tiny little scruffy mess and really unkempt. He was staggering around, staring listlessly at the wall just like you might expect any human who had been assaulted to behave. He'd clearly been slashed and beaten and all the people at the school who had seen him being brought in to safety were speculating as to what might have happened.

We heard there had been a party about a hundred yards from the school, just the night before the dog was found. There were pretty sketchy types apparently, and really drunk people everywhere, I was told, so maybe this poor dog had walked into this party at the wrong time and then emerged from there. Who knows? Someone else thought they had seen unfamiliar vehicles around that night, so they were guessing that maybe he'd been dumped by people driving through. It's impossible to really know what the truth was, but I certainly knew I didn't like the way this animal was behaving.

I wasn't fully sure but it seemed to me to be some sort of head trauma of some sort. He was staggering around as if he was drunk, wobbling headfirst into walls, falling over, his legs buckling from under him, the odd whimper coming from him. I just shook my head in despair. *There's no hope for this poor soul. This dog is done.*

This wasn't going to be a dog that I'd ever share online. His story was grim and depressing and I doubted he'd make it 24 hours. There are many dogs like this one that we quietly deal with and help as best we can but there's no point telling people all the sad stories.

All I could do was scoop him up and put him in the car and see what would transpire.

I spent the whole ride back thinking that this poor dog had had his chips, to be honest. But when we got him home to the land we started to look him over carefully, from nose to tail and see what, hopefully, we could clean up or bandage up and at least make him comfortable.

His fur was so matted with blood that we had to shave his head to allow us a better look at his wounds, and then once we saw, things truly looked horrendous. His head was slashed open in three places, and it was clear that although he was little he was quite an old dog. Frankly, he looked as sorry as I have ever seen a street dog look. My heart bled for the fella.

As we were trying to tidy him up and show him some love, it started to dawn on us that maybe some of his unco-ordinated staggering might actually be because of his poor sight, as well as the head trauma. Sure enough, when the vet gave his eyes a proper inspection it turned out he had cataracts and was probably about 90 per cent blind. He wasn't a young pup either, but quite an old boy.

All these things really just made me think yet again that it was the end of the line for this dog. However, we cleaned him up and agreed we'd observe him for a few days at the sanctuary and see how best to take things forward after that. I suspected it was more of a palliative care case.

What happened over those few days is something I had never seen in all my years of looking after injured and unwell street dogs: he started to *really panic* all the time. We tried loads of things to calm him down, like taking him out for little walks on the lead, gently offering him treats and speaking soothingly to him, but he often became quite frantic. He was just inconsolable.

Eventually, through trial and error, we figured out that the only way he would calm down is if we held him. So we would hold him for an hour, tight and close to our chests, and then he would slowly relax, but as soon as we set him down, he would quickly be off again into a panic. He would get so worked up and anxious that sometimes I worried he was going to have a heart attack or a stroke. We tried all sorts of things. First, we played classical music (sounds mad perhaps, but I promise it can help), then we had to feed him some calming tablets from the vet. They weren't heavy duty ones – I think they were just antihistamines which can sometimes do the trick. But none of this really relaxed him for a decent period of time.

The poor thing would always revert to being frantic once he wasn't being held close by us.

Over the next few days, through a pretty painful period of trial and error, we worked out that the only way to soothe him for a good long period was to take shifts and hold him until he fell asleep. We would take two-hour shifts each: I would do two hours, then everyone else who was around would cycle through doing their shifts too. We were passing him around from one to the other like I imagine parents do if their baby falls asleep on them.

After a while, and having talked it through with the vets, we realised this poor dog had post-traumatic stress disorder. Similar to humans, she explained to us, dogs can develop PTSD after experiencing distressing incidents, and therefore his attack, coupled with the fact his other senses were heightened from his blindness, meant he was at really high risk. In retrospect, he was showing all the classic symptoms of hypervigilance, aggression, reduced sleep as well as poor eating – even if we tempted him with our lovely fresh food. The vets described that hypervigilance is an exaggerated state of alertness, and manifests in dogs as restlessness, heightened startle responses and difficulty relaxing, which was basically a word for word description of his behaviour.

Thankfully, he seemed to calm down over a further week or two with us. He still wasn't great, but his cuts healed up and he was starting to regain his balance. Watching him improve, I was reminded of a boxer. He had been punch drunk and wounded coming straight out of a fight, but slowly he had begun to sharpen up and reclaim his faculties.

As he got a bit better, I started to think there was enough hope of him surviving that we ought to give this little dog a name. As soon as I thought this, his name was obvious, so we called him Billy. This was my grandfather's name and the two of them shared some lovely characteristics. They were both kind, little old gentlemen. It was the perfect name.

Given how much Billy had improved and responded, we wondered if there was anything else we could do for him that would allow him to get better. We had another dog going to the hospital, with Sybille taking him for an operation, so I said, 'Let's not give up on him, let's send Billy too.'

The hospital was 800 km away, which is the distance from London to the Scottish Highlands, so a decent journey for anyone, let alone a little blind dog with PTSD. Perhaps it was madness, and in retrospect the journey sent him spiralling back to his old frantic ways. It shouldn't have surprised me. However, the reason we sent Billy to the hospital was because I felt, and poor Sybille who must have found it incredibly stressful, agreed that Billy needed a specialist brain scan. We didn't have the facility to do an

MRI like that on the island, but we felt it was necessary to see if he had significant brain issues after his horrible attack.

The MRI result confirmed Billy had the cataracts but more importantly, it showed that he had brain swelling. 'Cerebral oedema secondary to traumatic brain injury' to give it its longer name. They looked after him for 10 days in the hospital and Billy calmed down again as the PTSD came under control. Some special treatment brought the brain swelling down too so that was great, and I was over the moon that he made the long journey back to us in one piece.

Although it was great to have him back, it felt like a kind of crunch time to assess what to do with Billy. I was attached to the old guy. And I felt ready by then to share his story online, with some of the key details: that there was an operation he could have to remove his cataracts and fix his eyes, that this would cost about $2,000, and that the earliest date for this was in about a month. I think I also mentioned that he would need a few follow-up appointments after the operation, which would drive the cost up further.

It wasn't so much begging as sort of trying to get other people's opinion on here was a dog in need, and what should I do? And should I really just focus on the hospital and the sterilising programme that was doing so well and the real key to the much bigger picture?

But much to our joy and amazement, someone came forward, a wonderful anonymous person on the other side of the world to us, and they promised to pay for the whole operation and aftercare. Staggering. So we booked Billy in. He went to the hospital four times in the end. Doing that huge journey. But he was such a sweetheart he deserved that chance. We had all bonded with him so much after holding him so close to us during his traumatic PTSD episodes.

As he recovered from the PTSD and settled into his personality, Billy proved to be actually really calm and mature and loving. Despite the abuse he became incredibly trusting. As a result, for a couple of the journeys we even let him travel on his own in a taxi. The transformation was unreal. He had a little suitcase that was bright royal blue with a 'B' embossed on it. We would pack this up with bandanas, blankets, brushes, grooming gear and, most importantly, treats, and then put him in the car like one of those old fashioned unaccompanied minors on aeroplanes. At the other end, the medical team would meet him like a distinguished returning visitor.

I realised that was stressful for him, but it was the only way that we could get him to the only place where they had the right set-up to get him better. And over the course of five or six months, we really *did* get Billy better. Seeing him get stronger, and almost younger, was unbelievable. Once he fully recovered from all the medical care, we concentrated on grooming him up. With care, better nutrition and love, his coat became a beautiful salt and pepper grey. He started to wear a little bandana, and he looked like a proper distinguished gentleman. He really did become a spiffing little dog. Everybody adores Billy!

The fact that the operation recovered his sight was a big thing for him. There was no way the procedure was guaranteed to be a success. But Billy recovered about 80 per cent of his sight, 100 per cent in one eye, and about 60 to 70 per cent in the other, and this meant he could properly see the world around him again. And it was in huge thanks to the donor who paid for him to have Billy's second chance.

When Billy first came back from the hospital in the taxi when he was able to see, I had one of those moments that really affirms to me that what I do is an utter joy. He'd become friends with Sandy and a few of the other dogs through his initial recovery. But he had obviously never been able to see me or Sybille or anyone else on the team who had saved him and held him when he was traumatised.

So when he came back and he could see us all, it was honestly just like a little miracle. After that, he really went on a voyage of discovery. I could have watched Billy all day looking out at the flowers and the other dogs and playing, just re-learning what the world looked like. It was almost like he knew he should have been dead, and he would have been. He wouldn't have survived for more than a couple of days on the streets after a vicious attack like that. He couldn't see, he was falling over and he would have been hit by a car, or starved because he wouldn't have been able to find his own food. Instead, his sight had returned, his PTSD had gone and he had a second chance in life.

Even better, we were delighted for Billy when we found a wonderful family from Singapore to adopt him. He moved there to a lovely big house, to live out his retirement and his twilight years in real comfort. As an older dog, maybe of eight or nine years, it's wonderful knowing he will have a good few years of truly loved life left in him. To this day, I have no idea where he came from, no idea of his backstory, or how he ended up outside that school with those injuries. I won't lie and say it was easy with Billy. It was hard in the early days, and I definitely doubted and reflected on the decision to spend that money and the time on him, when he was so unwell at the beginning. But now, I have absolutely no doubt it was the right decision, and that Billy is going to have the happy life he always deserved, being cherished and looked after.

With Billy settled I really wanted our loving little Buster – the mean-looking pitbull with the most adorable personality – to get his own happy ending too. As Buster had improved, the original owner would still be messaging me asking 'How's my dog?' In the beginning it was easy to stall him as Buster was still being treated and looked after.

But after about three months, by which time the guy had come to see Buster looking healthy and cured of his infections and his nasty ear haematoma, the situation really required some diplomacy. There was no way we wanted him to have to return to that horrible chain and damp concrete. Over my dead body.

So we used a mix of saying that Buster was still recovering and that he needed more time, and then we began to talk a bit more about the money we had spent treating and caring for him, and we teased it out for longer and longer. Eventually I think the guy got bored with us stalling and spooked by the money we had spent and he left Buster with us.

I'd also been worrying that he needed a home for a good few months now. But I also was aware that wouldn't be as straightforward as Billy's placement.

Two issues made me think this wasn't going to be easy. Firstly, a young pitbull with a chequered history, who was lacking half an ear, wasn't going to appeal to quite a lot of potential owners. Secondly, his breed isn't allowed to fly. The flat noses they have and how they breathe means they might run into difficulties getting enough oxygen up in a plane, so Buster would need to be found his forever home somewhere else in Thailand.

It had taken a good few months, but eventually the universe took some pity on poor old Buster. And a wonderful woman, Kitty, who is half Thai and half Finnish, came over and said she'd like to meet him.

Kitty stayed with us for quite a while the day she came. She had lunch, told us how she had recently lost a dog she loved so much and she spent some time alone with Buster. She was very thoughtful and considerate, and wanted to be sure that she could give Buster a good life and the right life for him before she made any firm commitment.

And after falling in love with his adorable personality, Kitty decided that, yes, she would take him and, oh my goodness, her and Buster have turned out to make such a wonderful partnership. Kitty is a tennis coach in Phuket, another island about four hours away, and Buster goes to work with her. I don't know if he collects the balls or just watches the play! They do all sorts together: they go on hikes, they go camping, he has outfits – a tuxedo and a rain jacket – that he dresses up in and he sleeps in bed with her. He really is the most spoiled, big, soft dog that you've ever come across.

It hasn't all been plain sailing for them though. About a month after he went to live with Kitty, Buster had an epileptic fit, and then a few more. Kitty and I were messaging back and forth over this terrible new turn of events. Happily, however, once the vet had looked Buster over and carried out some tests it wasn't all doom and gloom for

Buster. These days he's settled on medicine to keep the fits at bay and is once again the loveliest and most contented dog you could see.

I often think of him looking so pitiful on that chain leading a horrendous life of starvation, but he's never once looked back. As soon as he was free he simply decided, 'I'm ready to have the best time in life!' But then I think that if us humans had been kept like that, we would spend so much time being angry and grieving for a life we could have had. But Buster is just living in the moment and taking advantage of his new and joyful life. He's landed on his big, beautiful paws and he's the best goofball you ever could meet.

CHAPTER TWENTY

ALBA AND HER 14 BEAUTIFUL SUNSETS

When the alarm clock goes off in the morning, the first thing I do is a quick scan to see if there are any emergencies or dogs in need. That's when I saw it. The picture that was sitting in my WhatsApp still sends shivers down my spine. It was a horrid image of the skinniest dog I have ever seen in my life. Just like Tina, she appeared to be chained up and seemed to be disappearing into the ground.

I've never moved as fast in my life, pulling my shorts and t-shirt on as I replied to the message asking for location details and background on the dog. Two hours later we were driving through the jungle desperately looking for a little shack, stopping a few times to ask people if they knew the dog we were looking for. By now we knew the dog had been chained up and used as a guard dog or deterrent at a rural house. We'd already found the owners via some back channels, but they told us that the dog was fine and that we shouldn't touch it. They lived far away and only came back every two weeks to bring it food, as far as we could figure out. It was a dire situation but myself and Earth, who is our Thai videographer, chose to ignore all that advice and got on with trying to find the dog.

When we finally located her we noticed that the chain was old and rusty. She was sitting on a chair. She had some filthy rainwater and some dry food which was being eaten by ants and which she had lost interest in. She was a picture of absolute despair and looked like death warmed up. I've no idea how she was even still alive and was frightened to think how long she had been tied up. If the chain was anything to go by, I'd guess it was a very long time.

As we approached, she let out a little high-pitched bark which made my heart sink as much as it scared me. This poor creature was completely broken physically but it also seemed gentle and kind to the touch. A gust of wind could have blown her away.

What followed was frantic negotiation over the phone with her so-called owners. We stood firm. We said we were taking her and would return her when better. Myself and Earth both agreed that no matter what happened we wouldn't be returning her. We'd work it out later, but first we had to make an emergency trip to the vets.

She was in a bad way, that much was clear. It was easier to list what conditions she didn't have rather than all the ones she did. Her illnesses ranged among the most serious imaginable: heartworm, weak kidneys, severe anaemia, blood parasites, liver infection to a handful of other smaller conditions such as overgrown nails and malnutrition. She was covered in ticks and fleas and seemed incredibly weak.

We brought her back to Happy Doggo Land where we started to get her settled in, but I took one look at her and worried she would die that night. I didn't want her to die there alone in a little suite at the land feeling confused. She needed love and warmth in her life which is why I brought her back to my house to stay with me and Hank.

That first night she was way too frail to do anything except drink some water and have some fresh meaty bone broth which she lapped up before finding a little corner on the sofa that would quickly become her area. Nurse Hank sprang into action and sat watching her all evening long. He is a calming presence with the sick dogs and rather than sit beside me at my desk, which he almost always does, he protected our guest all evening long in a gentle and loving way.

I still believed there was a high chance that she could die that night so with her safely tucked in and surrounded by love, I sat down with the laptop for a very important task ... finding her a name. It's normally something I do quite quickly, but I spent a good hour looking at options. She deserved something very special.

I finally settled on the name Alba because it meant sunrise or dawn in both Italian and Spanish. I thought to myself, if I can get her a few sunrises it would be the perfect name for her. That night I left my bedroom door open so I could peek out at her from my bed. I tossed and turned all night long, and kept peering out to the sofa to see how she was doing. It was then that I saw Hank doing the same. He was sitting next to Alba on the couch watching over her.

By morning I couldn't wait to get up from my restless sleep. I found her in the same spot, and she'd made it through her first night. I gently carried her down the stairs to show her the first sunrise she'd had since freedom. Because she was so frail and sick I didn't want to do too much with her, as the horrible grey metallic collar was still gripping around her neck from the chain and her nails were so long that she struggled to walk without being in pain. Despite all that, myself, Alba and Hank all watched the sunrise beside my house before we retreated back inside for the dogs to have breakfast and continue their rest.

Miraculously, little Alba started to perk up. She had so little energy but what power she did have seemed to go into her tail and wagging it furiously any time she saw a human or Hank. I'm not sure she had ever known love or kindness in her life, but she was certainly open to receiving it even in this poor state.

I started to do small things for her like clean the ticks and fleas off her one by one. Because she was so weak we were very limited in the medicines we could try using as they could kill her, so it was all about taking a very softly, softly approach. Along with the horrible ticks being removed from her the most satisfying thing had to be getting a soapy wet cloth and gently washing the metallic grey from her neck. These were small and superficial things when compared to her bigger health issues, but they made not just Alba but the rest of us feel good. As I placed a little purple bandana on her neck which would become her beautiful signature look, I could see a little sparkle in her eye and Alba's dignity coming back.

Having learnt from Tina that you have to be very careful feeding a malnourished dog back to health, I set about giving Alba tiny portions. I wanted to get the very best food I possibly could so found a local café that had fresh organic chicken, which was cooked sous vide, and lightly poached salmon. It cost an absolute fortune, and was the sort of food I think millionaires eat, but I wanted to get only the best for Alba. She seemed to absolutely adore the salmon in particular and we started to slip some of her initial medicines into the food.

As the days passed I started taking Alba to see both the sunrise and the sunset. We'd cut her nails by this stage, and with four to five small meals per day I could even see a small bit of weight going onto her. It might only have been an ounce or two under her already tiny frame but I could feel progress.

Gradually, she started almost floating and skipping along with a new found freedom and confidence. There were some days I carried her up to a little rock about a hundred yards from my house where we would sit for ten to fifteen minutes and watch the sunrise. Her tail would always be wagging and her little eyes scanning the huge valley of palm trees and jungle in what seemed like disbelief. She was on top of the mountain commanding a beautiful view and the sun shining down on her body. Alba felt alive.

As we walked back to the house Alba would often stop as dogs do to smell whatever it is that has caught their attention. With her it was always the flowers. I would take a seat and watch her gently smelling the jungle flowers with her wonderful subtle mannerisms, her slightly upturned nose and her little goofy smile. It felt like watching some sort of little earth angel who was so happy with the simple things in life.

We made steady progress, but the reality was that Alba's body was too sick.

Her mind was still active and her will to live so strong. At a follow-up test with the vets the results were so bad, and looking at the graphs in disbelief the vets had no idea how she was still alive. Vets have a very careful way of phrasing things in a sort of coded language that doesn't quite say the dog isn't going to make it but at the same time not giving you any false hope. In Alba's case, I was so blindly invested in her future and drawn in by my love for her that I chose to sort of tune out from their warnings. Alba was safe now and we would get her better, I kept telling myself.

After about eight days with me, Alba took a turn for the worse and stopped eating. She was rejecting anything I brought her. I tried everything from kidneys and liver to fish and steak. Fresh prawns and rice. There wasn't a food type that I didn't try. I should have known that she wouldn't eat anything when she turned her nose away from her beloved salmon. Her body was shutting down.

Despite all the signs I continued to refuse to accept what was clear evidence right in front of me. Sybille made a visit and after trying some different things and looking at test results she lowered her voice and said, 'Alba's not going to make it, Niall.' Again I didn't really listen. As I saw Sybille's car leaving I changed Alba's bandana to a lovely fresh one and we went out to watch the sunset together. I told her all those people were wrong. The vets, Sybille, the test results and all the evidence. 'We'll beat this, Alba.'

And later that evening, I was jumping for joy when Alba finally ate some tuna. I'd nearly given up on her eating, but it finally worked. Not only did she eat it but as I went to bed with the door open she kept it down. We all woke the next morning and to my utter amazement she ate some more. Her tail wouldn't stop wagging. I went off to run some quick errands with my mind absolutely buzzing. Alba was a medical miracle.

After that moment of elation, I came home and started to try do a few little jobs around the house. The place was upside down with all Alba's little treatments and blankets and other bits. As I moved her sofa back to sweep away some fur my heart sank and my world collapsed … I found two tiny little mounds of fresh tuna that hadn't even been 1 per cent digested. She'd quietly puked them back up almost instantly without me seeing them.

In these moments I tend to switch to autopilot mode. I stared out the window and thought for a second. *What's the next move?* All I could think about was Tina and her hammock and the beautiful moments we had shared there together. Alba had been too frail for it but I decided that was where we had to go. I picked her up and walked out onto my balcony with her.

As we lay in the hammock, the sun was about to start its last hour of setting and sinking into the horizon. The view from my balcony is not as good as the one from the rock, but I thought this was the perfect spot for today. Alba was weak, I was sad and we just needed to switch off from the world. I put on Alba's song on repeat, an Italian song called 'Sarà perché ti amo', and we sunk deep into the hammock.

I never show any emotion in these moments as I feel like the dog is relying on me to be strong. There's plenty of time in the future for me to be sad or cry, but right there and then I needed to put my strong face on and pretend everything was going to be alright.

With the heat of the day fizzling out beautifully and the Italian 1980s pop music gently drifting across the valley, I started to talk to Alba. I knew it would be her last sunset. The only thing I knew to talk to her about was Tina. I told Alba how much she reminded me of the greatest girl there ever was. I kept my voice very upbeat and joyful, as if I was telling a child the happiest bedtime story in the world.

I explained to Alba about all the things that had happened since Tina had left us. About the 50,000 dogs we sterilised in 2024. About the trucks down at the land pouring concrete and laying electric cables for Tina's Hospital. I told her about all the people with ill health that Tina had given hope to over the last year. About the kind people climbing mountains in her name and raising money for her hospital.

I realised that I probably had never spoken about Tina like this before and so openly. About what an impact she'd had. I told little Alba that she would be seeing Tina sometime soon and that they would get on like the best friends in the world. Two sisters who would look out for each other and be the inspiration for so much of our work.

I told her that I know sometimes humans can be a little cruel and that she had been on the end of that cruelty, but that because of Tina's story and Alba's the world is changing. She would be waiting up there for her tomorrow and they could compare bandanas and enjoy their lives together.

As the sun started to set I could feel Alba's heart beat close to mine. It was highly irregular and skipping beats.

Her bones were angular and her suffering was a thing of the past. It was time.

I'm not a religious person, but I am somebody who believes in karma. I think whatever good you put out into the world comes back to you in some way. It might not be in the short term or even in your own lifetime, but I have to believe in something.

For that very reason, as I sat there with Alba in my lap and Hank now beside me as the sun set and the music played on as we all spoke with Tina, I felt a sense of pure contentment and calm. Hank had a horrible start to life, but here he was acting as a nurse for sick dogs. Tina and Alba had both been chained yet enjoyed immense joy and happiness in the short closing chapter of their lives. Then add me, I'd spent 42 years as a deeply unhappy person suffering from depression, addiction and anxiety. You couldn't come across a more broken bunch of souls, but here we were all making the most of our lot and helping each other in unimaginable ways.

Alba passed the next morning surrounded by all the loving faces who had helped her, including Hank. As she took her last breath I lent down and whispered into her ear to tell Tina her work down here is just starting and to look after little Alba for me.

THE END

WHO ARE YOU?

I post a lot online about the dogs' lives. That's because they're my passion and my purpose in life. But myself? And my own life? I don't post about that, other than the basic facts that, I think, inform why I do this. I was an alcoholic. I was addicted to pills. I'd got to the stage where I didn't see the point of life. I've always believed that being honest about some of my ugliest struggles in the past was important.

I often get asked questions about my life now, and it's not because I'm weirdly secretive that I don't post about myself. It's mainly because I think people find it boring. I'm often asked: Do I have a partner? Am I single? What do I do to unwind? Do I miss my friends and family? Am I lonely? Sometimes, people are wondering how they could make a similar lifestyle for themselves. But I'm happy to answer all of this, and share what my days out here actually look like … just be warned in reality it's possibly not as exciting as you might hope. (Sorry!)

TINA

Day-to-day life

Probably the first thing to point out is that I'm quite a maniac with my time; that's how I get things done. I'm very goal-oriented and once I'm focused on something I need to do then I'm ruthless about disregarding anything that gets in the way.

I'm always up early – just before 6 a.m. usually – and it takes me about a minute to shower. I can't stand wasting time beyond being clean and ready for the day. I've got no hair to fuss around with, and I just use clippers to shave it myself. Quick, free, no fuss. Same for brushing teeth. As for laundry, I've told you before how limited my wardrobe is: I just don't care about what I look like, so I see every second spent doing these daily things as a waste of my time. Hygiene is crucial, vanity is not.

I start work about a minute after I wake up. Either out the door to the land to open up and let the dogs out (this is a better morning), or I'll be checking my phone for emails and messages to fix problems with the Happy Doggo team around the world.

There is one ritual I have every single morning. Once I've finished the dog-feeding round, I drive past a little local shop – the very place where I bought my last ever bottle of whisky, on the same morning before I went to hospital.

That day, I recall I only had the equivalent of around five pounds in loose change, as I'd lost all my wallet and bank cards. I was shaking violently with tremors, tears were streaming down my face and I felt convinced I was going to die. Once I'd handed over the cash, I could barely carry the bottle in my hands as they were shaking so much. But when you're at rock bottom like I was, that whisky was needed to steady the nerves just to get to the hospital.

I now make a point of driving past that little store every day, come rain, sun or storms, and I smile to myself. Some days I wait until I am just around the corner and I punch the air down low by my side. It's a few seconds of happiness which reminds me daily just how far I've come. I don't take my sobriety for granted. It's a small, secret little routine that is important to me before the rest of the day takes hold.

Most of the stuff that comes with the dogs I can tolerate and get on with, but more than anything to do with this life it's the meetings that I hate the most. I really do despise them. I guess I'm more of a 'doer' than a 'talker'. Obviously, I know these meetings are needed for team work, and are essential to build our systems and processes and make all the big decisions and dreams I have become a reality. It's just that I'm so naturally impatient … I find it difficult to sit in one place and sometimes can be prone to overthinking things. Now this is something that I think many can secretly agree with so I hope I am not offending anyone but I find any meeting extremely painful. I'm able to get through them of course. I've sat through and led hundreds over the years, both in this role and in my previous careers, but that doesn't mean I don't feel like they're killing me inside. Sounds dramatic I know, but I'm just telling you the truth.

I calculate everything I do with one simple question: 'Will this help more dogs?' Like I said, if the answer is: 'Yes, it will', then I will do it. If the answer is: 'No, it won't help more dogs', then I don't care who it is, or what it is for, I won't do it. It's that simple. I even drive fast on my bike or semi-jog home just to not lose too much time. I'll leave food unfinished in restaurants or sometimes rush out of unimportant chats. That makes me sound terrible, doesn't it?

I don't cook – ever or rarely – and I haven't in the three years since I've been helping the dogs. This sounds crazy to people considering I was once a professional chef, but I don't want to waste my time. Of course I still need to eat to keep up my energy, so I usually eat a huge breakfast from a café or patisserie. And even while I wait to be served, I'll still be answering messages, thinking about work and fixing dog problems as they come in on my phone and sorting out money for vets. I'll often skip lunch (or grab a chocolate bar and can of pop) and then dinner will also be shop bought. I genuinely think the only three times I've cooked in the last three years was making the dogs their annual Christmas dinner. Which goes down a treat for them and people love seeing it online.

People often ask, 'But when do you switch off, Niall, when do you socialise and have fun?' In truth, in the whole of 2024 I probably only did about ten social things. Nine of them were one to two hours long. Quick dinners. A breakfast gathering for my birthday, when someone brought a cake and some candles. Playing a board game with my friends. My social life is absolutely non-existent in any normal sense – but I am fine with that.

Other (normal) people dream of fancy holidays or just two weeks' lying on a sunbed. I get that but it's not for me. What I secretly daydream about is to escape it all and have an isolated three-week trip on the Trans-Siberian Railway, just reading books. Or going to work on cargo ships as a chef where I could spend six months at sea knowing not one single person. Solitude is the biggest thing I crave.

My daily life seems slightly manic, I know, and probably not good for me in the long run health-wise, but that's just how I am and how my life runs. I am obsessed with my mission. I genuinely can't help it.

I finish work about one minute before I go to sleep, after answering some last-minute social media comments or quick work requests. I don't tend to have too many issues falling asleep because by the end of the day I've happily exhausted myself!

So in answer to the main questions I get asked …

Yes I am single, happily so. I have absolutely no life outside of helping the dogs, and I rarely see my friends (apart from the odd board game and pizza night) and family! If it seems like I am always busy online and don't have much time to myself that's because that is exactly what my life is like. Help the dogs, eat, sleep and repeat. Happy days!

The honest reasons why I feel this way made these decisions about women, relationships and kids come in more complicated answers. And the truth in those answers is a little more nuanced. You don't need to be a psychotherapist to analyse them. Having my parents unexpectedly split up, then seeing my mum have the crap beaten out of her, and becoming an alcoholic with severe depression and anxiety for close to 30 years all had a massive impact on how I choose to live now.

Those things (or 'trauma' as therapists would say) all shaped me.

I'm a natural loner, but I don't mean that in a sad, unhappy way, I promise! The reason I enjoy the company of dogs so much and have dedicated my life to them is because they are loyal, simple creatures who live in the moment. A dog has never let me down or hurt me emotionally.

When I got out of ICU I did a lot of walking, a lot of soul searching and a lot of thinking. I had wanted to die. Life couldn't go on like this. I knew that.

During that year before I started helping the dogs, I'll be honest. I was lost. All I could focus on – and I mean this quite literally on some days – was putting one step in front of the other. My life was about staying sober, working on my anxiety and depression and trying to make my body healthy again. Sounds easy but it was a period of torture both physically and mentally. It's pretty hard to admit to yourself that you tried to kill yourself and find the right path? Where do you even start?

In my work to get sober – and remain sober – I first had to identify the triggers that made me drink and made my mood low. Some of this I did with the help of therapy, and some of it came simply with the passage of time and learning more self-awareness. I came to these three main trigger points:

1. Relationships with women
2. Watching sports and drinking
3. Having no purpose in life

It took me a while to identify these, but once I had I could go about fixing them. It might seem wild, and the same things might not work for everyone, but I actually found a solution for all three. And I've simply stuck to those solutions ever since …

1. I decided I would remain single and not have any more relationships in my life. Any that I had over the years started out wonderfully, but I just didn't have the mental

capacity for them to last … and they would end in tatters with life with me as an addict and the other poor person trying everything to help me. However, ultimately that person would be let down and hurt as I pushed them further away and put the barriers up.

I know it's very hard for most normal people to understand, but I decided that if I was to stay alive and to be healthy, my best chance of doing so was to be 100 per cent alone. I knew I couldn't drag somebody else down with me again because of my mental state and addictions. I've stuck to that. And I'm at peace with it.

2. If you follow me online you'd think I was socially outgoing and always laughing and joking with lots of friends. The reality is that it's just me talking into a little black box that is my phone. I avoid people as much as I can socially! Not because I don't like them – I just struggle with it. I used to use alcohol to mask these social insecurities. I was especially drawn to watching sports in bars – football, rugby, cricket, American sports, Aussie Rules. You name it, I'd watch it. It took me about 25 years to realise that it wasn't the *sports* I was so interested in, but rather the pints of beer, Camel Lights and *crucially* the escape from my own head that drove me to bars to watch them.

Now, there's nothing wrong with watching a game with a few beers for most people, but I'd start with a Saturday lunchtime kick-off and still be drinking 48 hours later with just a couple of naps in between. I had to decide to cut out watching all live sports as it was a trigger for me. The only exception now is Formula 1 which I watch on my laptop at home. That one has stuck, but no longer with a drink in my hand. I can get enjoyment just from watching.

3. Given my decisions about my relationship status, it was clear I wouldn't be having kids. But it goes deeper than that. I was so sick with my mental health at times – and so addicted to alcohol and pills – that I always said to myself I would be no fit father. I don't want to burden some poor innocent soul with my mental baggage and drag them down.

The meaning of life

I'm a deep thinker about the whole purpose of life. Why are we really here? It has to be more than for a fortnight's holiday in Spain every year, paying the mortgage and binge-watching Netflix after a weekend in the local pub. Surely there has to be more?

The only thing I could really see that could have serious meaning would be having children and family – I saw the happiness and fulfilment that this brought others. Given that that wasn't for me and that I'd already achieved relative success in working life and travelled a lot, then I knew climbing some career ladder was never going to bring me life purpose either. Material success means nothing to me in the long term.

I know that only if I had a genuine purpose would I be able to stay mentally fit, fight my demons and not want to die again.

It all feels very simple to read those three things which I identified and see how they could work, but believe me those conclusions didn't come easily. I knew that by making those changes, and adding in easier things like fitness, I might just have a chance of the second half of my life being a happy one. And after putting into action all of the above I finally did find my purpose in life … the street dogs. And my life is happy – even if people might not look at it that way or want it for themselves.

What I do to stay well now

I always keep my social media posts upbeat, because, as I often say, there's enough gloom and doom in the world already. But I know there are plenty of people like me who might struggle with their mental health, and I wanted to talk a bit about mine here.

I don't want to depress anyone, so if you've never suffered with anxiety or depression (and good for you, you lucky thing) then by all means feel free to skip to the next chapter. But lots of people write to me about mental health, or addiction, and I wanted to share what I've learned from decades of hard-won experience. I'm not a doctor so I'm in no place to give out medical advice. It's just what I've found, and what I do now (on the advice of my own doctor) so I'm sharing it in case it helps.

Today, I would say my mental health is good. But that can change quickly. Since quitting booze I generally feel so much less anxious. On a day-to-day basis I can function, and I love my life here in Thailand and have found my purpose. Yet bad days still happen. And my God, do I know what it feels like to not feel in control. Despair and feeling overwhelmed I am all too familiar with.

I've been very open about my past, and while I think there's no magical cure I *have* found some tools that I use to beat the black fog off as hard as I can. I'm never going to beat it 100 per cent, I've accepted that, and it's an ongoing battle.

When I was drinking I became addicted to Valium (or Xanax, a similar highly addictive drug more widely used in the USA).

I used to sort of vanish from my life and go and sleep a lot and mope around when I had depression. I'd want to take myself into a dark room and hide, but I've learned to be more proactive these day and I promise it makes a real difference.

Depression is everywhere in the world – in your family, in your workplace, in your circle of friends – but there is still a lot of stigma and shame attached to it. Even though we have got better in the last decade or so in being honest about it, I guarantee you there's people you know and are close to who are hiding stuff, whether it's panic attacks, or postnatal depression, or overwhelming grief, or secret addictions. Mine wasn't so secret by the end, as you now know.

Anyway, as I write this on my laptop in the office, I'm looking fondly at Mr Hank the Tank (as I call him) who's got a bad leg at the moment. Forgive the tangent that follows, but Hank is a remarkable dog. He is huge, probably part bully, Dogue de Bordeaux and some other breeds. He is a big gentle giant who loves humans and female dogs but has a very hard time with other bigger male dogs. He appeared just after the first book came out and presented himself to us with an almighty hole in his back. It was just below his neck and about the size of a cricket ball. You could have stuck your hand in there it was so big.

He'd obviously either been in a fight or been injured somehow. We found him in some kind of makeshift camp with a few other dogs who'd been in need of shelter during the monsoon season. (Unless you live out here, it's impossible to explain just how heavy the rainfall can be – a bucket could be overflowing within half an hour, and muddy tracks soon become like streams. Wooden shacks can be washed away. It's dangerous, for humans and dogs, if you're not careful.)

As a street dog, and in the humid, rainy season, the alarming-looking crater on poor old Hank's body was far from clean. As the wound was on his neck directly behind his head, he hadn't been able to self-clean with his tongue in any way like he might otherwise instinctively have tried to do. What this meant was that when I peered a little closer, I was horrified to see the hole was absolutely full of maggots. I kid you not, there must have been hundreds of the wriggling little larvae left by flies in there. The longer and more often that I looked, it seemed like they were multiplying. It was like some kind of horror movie or nightmare.

I'm used to seeing injuries by now, but this kind of stuff gives me the heebie-jeebies. The stink of rotting flesh. The wriggling. Poor Hank was literally being eaten alive by these disgusting maggots. They had to come out of his body – and soon.

My first concern in that instant, however, was how to approach this poor dog. He was built (excuse my language) like a brick sh*thouse. Or indeed a tank, which is how he got his name, Hank the Tank. I reckon he probably weighed in at about six stone. I assumed he'd be angry and vicious and might well try and take my arm off when I tried to approach him. I've learned the hard way to always try and think: how can I help, without actually losing my own limb here?

But, to my surprise, Hank seemed a friendly fella, the opposite of snarling or reluctant to be approached. That tough street survivor dude actually willingly ran over to us and practically jumped in the truck himself! He genuinely seemed to be saying to the other dogs lurking around curiously: This is my chance to get sorted out, guys – and I'm bloody well taking it.

Once at the vets, they started the laborious process of cleaning up the maggots, but his body was just exhausted. If you've got something nasty eating away at you, you're going be quite a sick dog.

Despite this, he had found himself a dwelling place in a sort of camp with other dogs. And it was the usual situation of us not knowing a thing about the backstory. There were a few different versions of the truth flying around. One was that he belonged to some foreigners originally who'd left him during Covid (which was plausible) and that these Thai people had then taken him in but he'd been left to his own devices. God knows how that explained the hole though.

We took him in immediately, and despite the fact he looked huge and aggressive, with me he seemed a big, goofy guy and actually very friendly. At the vets, several dedicated members of staff got to work picking the maggots out of his body one by one while he was given some sedatives to keep him calm.

It took about two hours to make any progress at all with clearing the cavity. I imagine having all these parasites feeding off your body is rather exhausting and your body becomes overwhelmed.

Each maggot was individually plucked from him, but once the wound is cleaned there are eggs that have been missed and then a new cycle begins. So you can't stitch up or mend the wound (or you'd trap them), and it usually takes about two or three visits to the vets over the course of two or three days to fully shift the little blighters. I was having a go at home with tweezers too, as much as I hated them and was grossed out, but I had to help poor Hank as much as possible.

Once he was cleaned up and in better health, Hank actually settled in well at the land. He was very good friends with some of the other dogs, like good old Cindy Crawford and especially the female dogs (male dogs together can cause more issues). He was sterilised and healthy enough once the hole had cleared up, though it had left his leg a bit dodgy which I feared would make him harder to adopt. Right, tangent over.

So as I was saying, I think it's helpful to try and tackle mental health in the same way as we mend physical ailments. There are treatments available and you shouldn't be ashamed to talk about it or seek help. Just because depression isn't visible, you shouldn't deal with it alone. Nor should you think everyone else's needs come first and you just have to soldier on.

I spend a lot of my time giving dogs medicines and taking them to vets and getting them physio or vitamins or anything I can really to get the dog better. And I know there are mums and carers who do the same all their waking hours – giving everything to the people they love and forgetting to look after themselves. Please, do start looking after yourselves. It's like when parents are urged to put on their own oxygen mask before their children on aeroplanes – you need to keep strong yourself in order to be able to help others.

Taking the meds

It's frustrating having depression. And it took me years to accept it. I blamed my drinking, or panic attacks, or just being moody. I've been on antidepressants before in my life and tried different ones. Some of them worked. Some of them didn't. Obviously, when you mix them with alcohol, as I did, they're a lot less effective.

I found an antidepressant that works for me. I take a pill every day. It's commonly prescribed all around the world and belongs to a class of drugs known as selective serotonin reuptake inhibitors (SSRIs) which work by helping to restore the balance of a serotonin (like a happy hormone) which is naturally found in the brain (and newer research seems to suggest the gut too).

I've taken them for three years now, since I stopped drinking and had my breakdown, and they do work. By and large, the only time I mess up is when I stop taking them. There are periods when I will miss two days in a row

– never on purpose, it's just that I'll forget to buy them in the chemists, or I'll just be distracted with work and I'll forget to take the tablets. But I've noticed that I can really feel the difference, and sometimes I can start having issues straightaway when that happens. My mood drops and I get very blue. Life feels more overwhelming.

So my antidepressant prescription is very important for me, but recently Sybille, my 'you can call her at any time' good friend out here who is a trained human doctor and who helps out with the dogs, talked me into getting a full health check-up.

Sybille is just brilliant by the way. She has a heart of gold and is without a doubt one of the kindest and most caring animal lovers I have ever met. She works part-time at a clinic on the island looking after people, but also cares for 20 (yes *20*) disabled dogs at her home as well as doing so much for us, like collaborating with local vets to coordinate care for the dogs, and taking the lead on diagnostics and treatments. So when Sybille gives me advice I do try and pay attention. Off I went for the check-up.

What was found was a bunch of chemical imbalances I didn't know I had. So now I also take other supplements and try to boost my body with nutrients I was missing. You may not believe in all that stuff, and that's fine, but when you've abused your body as much as I had all those years I figured it wouldn't harm me to try and boost myself with some of the good stuff.

Thanks to these supplements the improvement in my energy levels and mood is staggering. I'm actually bouncing around the place these days. That doesn't mean I am constantly happy; of course I still have little moments. But the vitamins, along with other healthy habits, have helped.

More importantly I want people to know that depression and anxiety are *illnesses*. If I got a whack on the head, I wouldn't just completely ignore it. If I needed fixing up like Mr Hank, I wouldn't refuse all medicines and think, *Oh, I hope I just get better.* No – you'd be taking what the doctor told you to. Try and see depression and anxiety like that. Guys are especially bad, I know, at shrugging things off, instead of seeking medical help. But it's so important.

If I'm honest I don't love the idea of taking tablets every day for the rest of my life (who does) but I accept that it's working for me and I'll stick with it.

Panic attacks

I thought panic attacks were caused by hangovers (which certainly don't make them any better and drinking makes these more likely – and more intense) and at times I genuinely believed I was having a heart attack.

You might think of a panic attack as the equivalent of being nervous about a football match, or an exam, or a driving test, or a job interview, or a first date.

That's definitely anxiety, and that's totally normal.

But those butterflies in your tummy? Those sweaty palms? I'm not belittling your experience as I know these symptoms are *not* fun. But I promise you, that's just not a panic attack. Panic attacks are at a level where you actually think you're dying.

For me, these happen when I'm overstressed, when I've worked myself up, and they can come out of absolutely nowhere. My heart will start beating a lot faster, my breathing will become really shallow, and I'll get what I can only describe as hyper-hyper-anxious feeling. It's entirely physically and mentally all-consuming.

A therapist explained it to me one time and her example really resonated with me. It was this: imagine you're driving in your car and you're about to hit a dog or a cat, maybe in the middle of the road, or even (God forbid) a small child. You'd instantly slam on the brakes, and your body would certainly go into a sheer and utter panic for the next five or six seconds while it tries to catch up with your brain's thoughts – your heart would be racing like galloping horses, you'd be sweating, you'd be (understandably) super-super-stressed. And it would be the most horrible feeling ever, right?

For a normal person, once you knew that the cat or dog or, God forbid, small child was actually safe, you'd experience that level of panic for five or ten minutes and then probably be able to reassure yourself the immediate danger had passed. *Everything is OK.*

Well, those sensations of sheer horror and panic are exactly how a panic attack in my world feels every time, without the jeopardy of running anything or anyone over to start it off.

And it lasts for anywhere between 30 minutes and four or five hours. It's truly hideous. I'm not saying this to get sympathy, more to try to explain what it feels like for people.

And then, because you've been so incredibly panicked, your body becomes completely exhausted and drained of its battery afterwards. Getting through the panic attack itself (no mean feat because you think you're going to die) is the first part, but then you're left feeling like you're good for nothing, because, no matter how many times you've had them, *you still think you're going to die.*

I had one recently, and I still thought to myself, *OK, that's it, Niall, you've done great with the dogs, your life's been good, but you're done here, fella.* Even though I've had so many in the past I still genuinely felt at that stage that I was going to die. It's 'just' a panic attack, sure, but you can't be logical in that moment when it's happening.

Hiding from the world

People who've got depression or anxiety will know that the very first thing we want to do is close the curtains and get into bed. And stay there. Shut out the world.

And if you know someone who gets like this, suffering from depression or anxiety, a really good tip would be to give them space, because that person is probably not able to do any more than climb into bed.

I feel physically sick from anxiety and depression, so closing the door is the first thing I do. Because hearing even an innocuous noise outside, like an exhaust pipe blowing, could set me off when I've got a panic attack, making me think the world is going to end or that somebody's coming to attack me and hack me into pieces or something like that. That's the level of anxiety you're operating at on those bad days. So often the bed is the place where you end up.

What makes it worse ... and what helps

The worst thing you can ever do is drink, for alcohol is like adding fuel to the fire of anxiety. Recreational drugs also wreck mental health. And self-medicating with prescribed pills like Valium or Xanax, which are a short-term relief for a panic attack, become a problem because they're massively addictive. I now stay clear of these; they're not a good solution in the long term. The worst 'comedown' I ever had was withdrawing from Xanax – it was like my skin was crawling. Horrific.

When you drink you forget about the anxiety and the depression for a bit, but then the next day it comes back five times worse, and you have to drink again to make the anxiety go away. So that's how I became an alcoholic. But even those who may be classed as normal people who have a dose of anxiety might be tempted to drink to escape their own head. It's definitely not worth it.

So my top tips are to avoid alcohol and drugs misuse.

Running

Exercise is an important part of my toolkit for staying calm. If I run 5k every day, I can almost guarantee that the next day is probably going to be OK, I'll feel more on top of life and sleep better. If you can grab a dog to take with you even better. But I run alone too to clear my head and see it like putting some fuel in my tank.

If 5k seems far too far, just go for a 2k walk. Or even shorter. Go and walk to the park, simply putting one step in front of the other and moving can help. I appreciate that not everyone is able to walk but doing anything that helps jolt you out of the present is good. I sometimes move my head from side to side and even that can give me the necessary break I need.

Massages

Getting the odd massage is a treat for me. They've got really good Thai massages out here (funnily enough) and I like the really hard ones where an old woman will seem to crunch my bones. It gives me a little reset.

Therapy

I've had this at different stages in my life and found it useful mostly. When I came out of hospital I had therapy via Zoom, but since I've been in recovery from drinking I haven't had any more.

Should I? Well, probably. I always blame being busy. Let's face it, therapy isn't exactly comfortable, no-one relishes it, but that's not the point. It's all about 'doing the work' on ourselves, and I get that.

I really did get a hell of a lot out of therapy, and it can save and change lives.

So I would recommend it, if you feel it would help you. The problem with me is that, because I'm kind of in a happy place mostly, I assume I don't need therapy at the moment.

But of course I realise I probably do! I should get more therapy. The only way I justify my decision not to be having sessions at the moment is because I have become much better at talking to my friends about my feelings and what's going on in my head. (Don't worry I also listen to them too, I don't solely bang on about myself.) And I'm much better at telling other people more when I'm actually sick and opening up about that.

There's no way I want to start drinking to the bottom of a bottle anymore because I sure as hell know the answers don't lie there. So not official therapy, but therapy by friends. I think it's just as important.

Meditation

Again this is something I've used before and it's a great tool to have in your kit.

I *should* practise it every day, or at least frequently, but I have to admit I only turn to meditation when I start to feel 'triggered' and start noticing the signs in myself that tend to mean my mental health is going downhill.

I get irritable and snappy as the anxiety rises up inside me when I'm very tired and very stressed, and my breathing gets more shallow. Then I know I need to take a few moments and meditation is handy. I usually do a body scan kind of meditation, which you can find on YouTube, and they're 20 or 30 minutes long which seems to slow my heart rate and breathing down. It can work miraculously well. If I wanted to be super-healthy, I would do 10 minutes every day, instead of just relying on it in times of trouble, because usually if I'm feeling the need to meditate I'm on a downward slope.

Sunshine helps

I know it's all very well for me to say this while I'm living on a tropical island (sorry), but part of the urge to move here was because I know I'm the sort of person who gets easily affected by the weather. When I lived in Ireland and especially when I lived in England, which constantly seemed to be rainy, it definitely affected my mood and brought me down.

So I've set myself up in life in a sunny place.

For me living somewhere where the sun shines means the culture is all about being outdoors. I take the dogs outside, whereas in England or Ireland when it's cold you easily end up in the pub. It's not so easy to find other things to do. So moving here has really helped that aspect of my life.

I hope that I will never drink alcohol again, and I've never been tempted to since I quit four years ago. But that doesn't mean I don't sometimes stand in the 7-Eleven store where I would have previously bought my booze and see the lovely cold beers in the fridge, and think how nice they look. You still can think this while feeling strong enough that you won't undo all the progress you've made.

But just because I've quit drinking doesn't mean I don't have any vices.

Nobody can be perfect all the time. I know that the perfect food for my brain might be salmon and avocado and raw vegetables, but I'm afraid my guilty pleasure is Thai-style fried chicken which is super-tasty and cheap. I also love chocolate – Kinder Buenos are my favourites at the moment – and fizzy pop. I'm afraid I have at least one can of full-fat Coca-Cola a day. Yes, I know, it will rot my teeth and do my waistline no good. But the little treats in life keep us going …

ACKNOWLEDGEMENTS

To all the people who help me on the ground, including the Happy Doggo team and Valeria and Sybille. I want to especially thank Lindsay, who never wants any credit or limelight but who is responsible for so much of what we achieve with Happy Doggo.

We wouldn't be able to do what we do or even think of building a hospital were it not for the help and support we have. I couldn't single out one individual donor, but to the people who send $4 instead of having a Starbucks, or the children who send their pocket money for the dogs, I am in awe of you.

Thanks to Susanna Galton and Ajda Vucicevic, who helped with the book over so many late nights. Also thank you to Simon Gerratt, Dani Mestriner, Daisy Ward, Hetty Touquet, Sarah Burke, Emily Langford, Shannon Branch and all at HarperCollins for their hard work in putting the book together. I was kicked out of school at 16 and never learned how to write or spell or any grammar, so they have worked absolute miracles in making this a book you can actually read and enjoy.

To my mum, dad, sisters and brothers, I know you see me so little and I should make more time. The mission I am on isn't easy for my friends and family, but they have only ever been supportive. To my two best friends Sean and Richard, thanks for the WhatsApp advice and jokes to keep me sane when things are tough.

I'm keeping this list short because there are literally thousands of people who help the dogs with me just acting as a conduit and getting all the acclaim. From donations to online shares to adopting dogs, there are so many ways in which so many people help.